☑ S0-AZG-475

DATE			

Endpaper: Midway Atoll, with Sand Island at left and Eastern
Island in foreground.

MIDWAY
Battle
for the
Pacific

Eighteen American warships and hundreds of American warplanes were destroyed or badly damaged in the Japanese attack on Pearl Harbor, and it would take months or years for American industry to replace them all. So in the spring of 1942 the commander of the U.S. Pacific Fleet, Admiral Nimitz, needed time.

But Admiral Yamamoto, who commanded the Japanese Combined Fleet, was eager to fight a major sea battle before the U.S. Navy could regain its strength. He planned to sink the remaining American warships after luring them into a trap—with the little islands of Midway as the bait.

In this book Edmund L. Castillo tells what happened when Admiral Nimitz's limited forces confronted the massive strength of the Imperial Japanese Navy. Captain Castillo also shows why Midway turned out to be the most important naval battle of World War II.

MIDWAY
BATTLE
for the
PACIFIC

Captain Edmund L. Castillo, USN

Illustrated with maps and photographs

RANDOM HOUSE • NEW YORK

The author gratefully acknowledges permission to reprint and to adapt one chart from *Midway: The Battle That Doomed Japan* by Mitsuo Fuchida and Masatake Okumiya. Copyright © 1955 by U.S. Naval Institute, Annapolis, Maryland.

All the photographs in this book are from the U.S. Navy with the exception of the following: U.S. Air Force, 57, 88; U.S. Marine Corps, 74, 86 (both).

Maps, decorations, and design by Ted Burwell

Library of Congress Catalog Card Number: 68–14485

Manufactured in the United States of America

For JIM

Contents

Maps and Charts

MIDWAY
Battle
for the
Pacific

Wildcat

1.

Pacific Outpost

Midway is the name of an atoll, a nearly circular coral reef and two small islands, perched on top of an underwater mountain in the central Pacific. It is 1140 nautical miles from Pearl Harbor, 2250 from Tokyo, and about 3000 nautical miles from the west coast of the United States.

Midway is an uninviting place. It has no native inhabitants, no industry, and no natural resources worth mentioning. Until the early 1900s, when Americans planted a tough California beach grass and a few trees, practically nothing grew in the dry, sandy soil of the two islands. Midway has no natural source of fresh water—nothing, in fact, to recommend it at all, except a strategic location in the middle of the Pacific. Midway is a place most visitors would be happy to forget.

But Midway will not be forgotten. It cannot be, for more than 3000 Americans and Japanese died there, and in the waters nearby, in the most important naval battle of World War II.

Atlases show Midway as part of the Hawaiian chain. Technically, at least, the atlases are right. Midway's mountain base is part of a range of volcanoes that burst out of the sea in prehistoric days to form the islands that now make up the state of Hawaii. But there the resemblance ends. The Hawaiian Islands rise high out of the water. Their mountain peaks tower thousands of feet above the sea. Over the ages, lava from their smoking craters turned into fertile soil. Then lush, green plants, tall trees, and the twisting vines of a tropical jungle grew to cover the sides of the majestic mountains and the beautiful plains below. When man arrived, he began to tame the jungle, eventually replacing much of it with cities, towns, and huge plantations of pineapple, sugar, and coconut palm.

Midway is no such paradise. At Midway the mountains stayed below the sea. Only the peak of one volcano rose near enough to the surface for sunlight to filter down to it. Tiny marine animals, called polyps, attached themselves to the circular lip of the dimly lit volcano crater, and deposited limestone. They died, and other creatures followed them. Gradually, over a period of many thousand years, they built the top of the mountain higher, as generation after generation of the tiny underwater creatures formed layer after layer of hard, porous coral.

Finally the ring of coral reached the surface of the sea. Since the creatures that built it live only in salt water and cannot exist in the air, the mass of coral stopped growing upward. There it remains, in some places just above the surface, in others just below it, nearly circular in shape, like the crater of the volcano on which it stands.

Inside the coral reef is a shallow lagoon, about six miles across. In the lagoon, along the slightly flattened south side of the reef, lie the two islands. They, too, are made of coral, which has crumbled to form a coarse, brilliant white sand. The sand is so white that Marines stationed there during World War II often were burned *under* their chins by the bright, tropical sunlight reflected up from the ground.

Sand Island, the larger of the two islands, is irregularly shaped. It is almost two miles long and about a mile across at its widest point. Sand Island's largest "hill" stands 39 feet above sea level. It is the highest point of land for several hundred miles.

Eastern Island is roughly triangular. Its longest side is about a mile long, and the island is nowhere more than about a half-mile wide. Eastern Island is nearly flat. It rises at most only 12 feet above the Pacific.

Polynesian fishermen probably knew of the islands centuries ago, but the atoll was not formally "discovered" until 1859. In that year, an American captain sailing from Hawaii came upon the islands and claimed them for the United States. After the American Civil War, Midway was surveyed by the United States Navy. A channel was dredged through the reef and the lagoon made deeper, so that ships might enter and anchor there in the shelter of the reef.

In 1903 Sand Island became a station on the commercial cable line linking the Philippines with Hawaii and the west coast of the United States. A few employees of the cable company came to Midway to live. It was they who imported the grass and trees. From 1904 until 1908, the islands were guarded by a small detachment of United States Marines. Few Americans had heard of Midway, however, when Pan American Airways began development of the island as a commercial seaplane station in 1935. Pan American built a small hotel on the lagoon side of Sand Island, near the cable company's little settlement. On June 6, 1935, the first Pan American Clippers, long-range twin-engine passenger seaplanes, began making regular stops at Midway on their way to the Philippines and China.

In 1939 the United States began to fortify Midway. Progress was slow, and it was not until late 1940 that a Marine detachment of nine officers and 168 Marines, with a shore battery of two 5-inch guns, was permanently stationed at Sand Island. As war clouds gathered to the west, this force was increased. By December 1941, the Marine ground force numbered approximately 30 officers and 575 enlisted men. The shore battery boasted six 5-inch guns. A naval air station was built on Eastern Island that summer. Its three runways formed a triangle that occupied most of the little island. A squadron of Navy patrol seaplanes was stationed there, and a squadron of Marine scout bombers was scheduled to arrive on December 7, 1941.

Midway's Marines and Navy pilots learned by radio of the attack on Pearl Harbor that morning. Then orders came by cable telling the island commander to put his war plans into effect. This meant little more than digging foxholes, issuing ammunition, and turning out all the lights at sunset. The Marine scout bombers did not arrive that day. The aircraft carrier that was bringing them was sent, instead, to search for the Japanese fleet. That evening, a pair of Japanese destroyers bombarded the island. The bombardment killed four men and wounded ten. It also destroyed a seaplane and damaged a hangar.

During the weeks that followed, Midway received some reinforcements. Admiral Chester W. Nimitz, who assumed command of the Pacific Fleet on December 31, had little to spare, but Midway had suddenly become important. With the loss of Guam, Wake, and the Philippines, Midway was the last American outpost in the central Pacific, the only important American base west of Pearl Harbor. Nimitz was determined to hold it.

Chester Nimitz was a determined man. He was born in Texas, the grandson of a master merchant mariner, and graduated from the Naval Academy at Annapolis with distinction, standing seventh in a class of 114 midshipmen. Commissioned in the Navy in 1907, he spent his early years in battleships, cruisers, destroyers, and gunboats, before qualifying for duty in submarines.

In 1912, while commanding the submarine *Skip-*

Admiral Chester W. Nimitz, Commander in Chief, U.S. Pacific Fleet.

jack, Nimitz, then a lieutenant, was awarded a medal for saving the life of a seaman. The sailor, who could not swim, had fallen over the side and was being carried away by a strong tide. Nimitz dove in after him, fought the tide, and held him up until both could be rescued from the sea.

Later, during World War I, he was commended by the Secretary of the Navy for "meritorious service as Chief of Staff to the Commander, U.S. Atlantic Submarine Fleet."

After the war, as a captain, Nimitz commanded the cruiser *Chicago* and later the cruiser *Augusta*. He never commanded a battleship, a prize command most Navy captains sought in those days; but in 1938, after being promoted to the rank of rear admiral, he was given command of Battleship Division One, a group of three battleships. One of them, USS *Arizona*, served as his flagship. Another, USS *Pennsylvania*, was flagship for the Commander in Chief of the U.S. Fleet.

For many years, Nimitz had been known as one of the Navy's most brilliant—and at the same time most human—officers. He was a rear admiral with a desk job in Washington when the Japanese attacked Pearl Harbor. Ten days later, President Franklin D. Roosevelt promoted him over the heads of 28 other officers to the rank of four-star admiral and the post of CINCPAC—Commander in Chief of the U.S. Pacific Fleet.

Many years before, as a young officer, Chester Nimitz had faced a court-martial for running a ship aground. Few officers in any navy can expect much of a career after being brought before a court, even if they are acquitted of the charges. Nimitz not only was acquitted but went on to the highest rank in the Navy. Now as CINCPAC he faced a tough assignment. Much of his fleet was hard aground, sitting on the bottom of Pearl Harbor. What was left was spread distressingly thin over a vast ocean.

Nimitz was a gentleman—calm, quiet, considerate of his officers, and able, at the same time, to inspire them to work harder and better than they had ever worked before. He had a genius for organization, and at the same time was a shrewd tactician, a brilliant strategist, and an accomplished diplomat. He brought to the Pacific Fleet the kind of leadership it needed,

Captain Cyril T. Simard, commander of Midway Atoll.

at a time when leadership was desperately needed.

In the early months of 1942, Nimitz became convinced that the Japanese were planning an attack on Midway. On May 2, without any warning, he flew to Midway to inspect its defenses. There he met with Commander Cyril T. Simard, commander of the atoll, and Lieutenant Colonel Harold D. Shannon, commander of Midway's Marine garrison. Nimitz asked Shannon what he needed to hold the islands against a Japanese assault. Shannon quickly rattled off a list— more anti-aircraft guns, more riflemen, more barbed wire, and more aircraft, to mention just a few of the items.

"If I get you all these things you say you need," Nimitz asked, "then can you hold Midway against a major amphibious assault?"

"Yes, sir," Shannon replied.

In less than a week, the Marine riflemen, barbed wire, anti-aircraft guns, fighters, dive bombers, and other weapons were on their way. The Army Air Corps sent Simard 18 B-17 Flying Fortresses and four smaller B-26 bombers. To show his confidence in Simard and Shannon, Nimitz also saw that they both were promoted, Simard to Navy captain and Shannon to Marine Corps colonel. By the first week of June, there were more than 100 planes, 141 officers, and about 3000 enlisted men at Midway.

Admiral Nimitz emerges from an underground bunker into Midway's blinding sunlight.

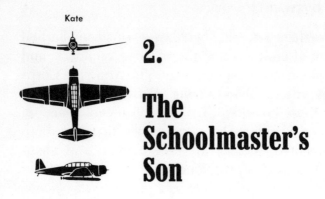
Kate

2.

The Schoolmaster's Son

Nimitz's adversary, on the other side of the blue Pacific, was Admiral Isoroku Yamamoto, Commander in Chief of the Japanese Combined Fleet. (See the Appendix for the pronunciation of Japanese names.)

Yamamoto was the son of a village schoolmaster and a descendant of the samurai class, the warriors of feudal Japan. Although he grew up in an inland village, he applied for admission to Japan's naval academy. He took the entrance examination at the age of 15, expecting to fail, and scored second out of 300 applicants.

Japan was a backward country in Yamamoto's youth. Previous emperors and their warrior nobles had closed the country to foreigners for several hundred years. Now the Emperor Meiji was trying to open the country to new ideas, to force it out of the seventeenth century and into the twentieth in a period of only a few years. It was a time of great change.

Life at the naval academy was unbelievably harsh. Discipline was strict. Study hours were long, and physical demands were cruel. Midshipmen were required to swim three hours each day in the Inland Sea, and once a year they had to swim ten miles, from the island shrine of Miyajima to Etajima, the island where the academy was located. The long swim took as much as 13 hours. A tenth of the students left the school every year because of failing health. Three years were spent

Admiral Isoroku Yamamoto, Commander in Chief, Japanese Combined Fleet.

at Etajima. The fourth was spent aboard a full-rigged sailing ship, learning to battle the sea. The schoolmaster's son made the grade. Like Nimitz, Yamamoto graduated seventh in his class.

As an ensign, Yamamoto served in a cruiser during the Battle of Tsushima Strait. This great battle, which was fought in the narrow channel between Japan and Korea on May 27, 1905, brought Japan victory over Russia in the Russo-Japanese war.

During the battle Yamamoto's cruiser was hit. The young officer was knocked unconscious and woke up to discover that he was wounded in the leg and had lost two fingers from his left hand. He was thrilled by the battle and by his Navy's great victory, and he considered his own wounds to be of no importance. "When the shells began to fly above me," he wrote home to his family, "I found I was not afraid. . . . When victory was announced . . . even the wounded cheered." And well they might. Of the 27 ships making up the Russian fleet, 23 were sunk in the fierce battle. It was the first triumph for the new Japanese Navy.

During World War I, Yamamoto spent two years in the United States, studying at Harvard University. He became such an expert in the affairs of the American oil industry that several American oil companies offered him jobs. Later, from 1925 to 1927, he was his country's naval attaché in Washington.

During these two visits to the United States, Yamamoto grew to know and respect America and Americans. For many years he opposed the idea of war against the United States. "If it is necessary to fight," he told the Japanese prime minister, "in the first six months to a year of war against the United States and England I will run wild. But I must also tell you that if the war is prolonged for two or three years, I have no confidence in our ultimate victory."

Yamamoto was Vice Minister of the Navy when he said those words. In the next few months, his opposition to war with the United States became so strong that Admiral Yonai, his superior in the Naval Ministry, made him Commander in Chief of the Combined Fleet, chiefly to get him out of Tokyo. It was the only way Yonai knew to keep him from being assassinated by fanatical Army officers who had seized control of the government and were pushing Japan toward war.

Yamamoto was not pro-American, as some of the Army officers claimed. He was thoroughly pro-Japanese. But, unlike most officers of the Japanese Army, he had traveled to Europe and the United States. He knew enough about his own country and about the rest of the world to realize that Japan could not win a major war against industrialized nations. Japanese industry just could not build a war machine powerful enough to overcome the United States and Great Britain.

Once in command of the Combined Fleet, however, Yamamoto soon became convinced that war was unavoidable. From that time on, he devoted himself completely to strengthening the Japanese Navy and preparing it for war against the United States.

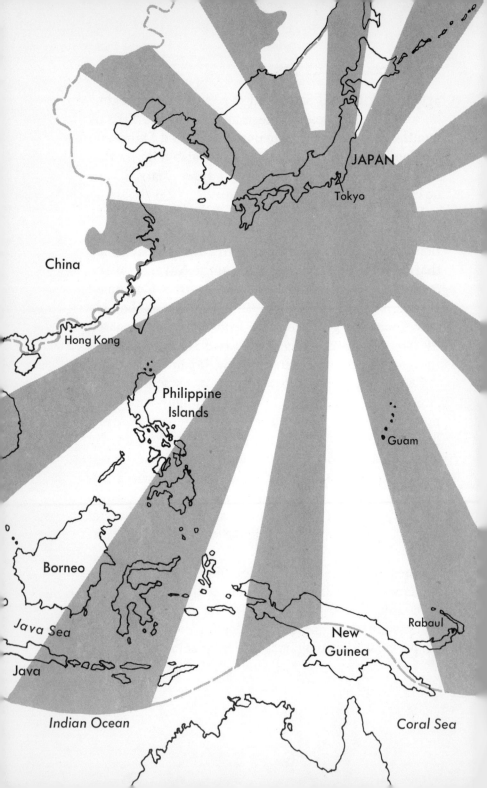

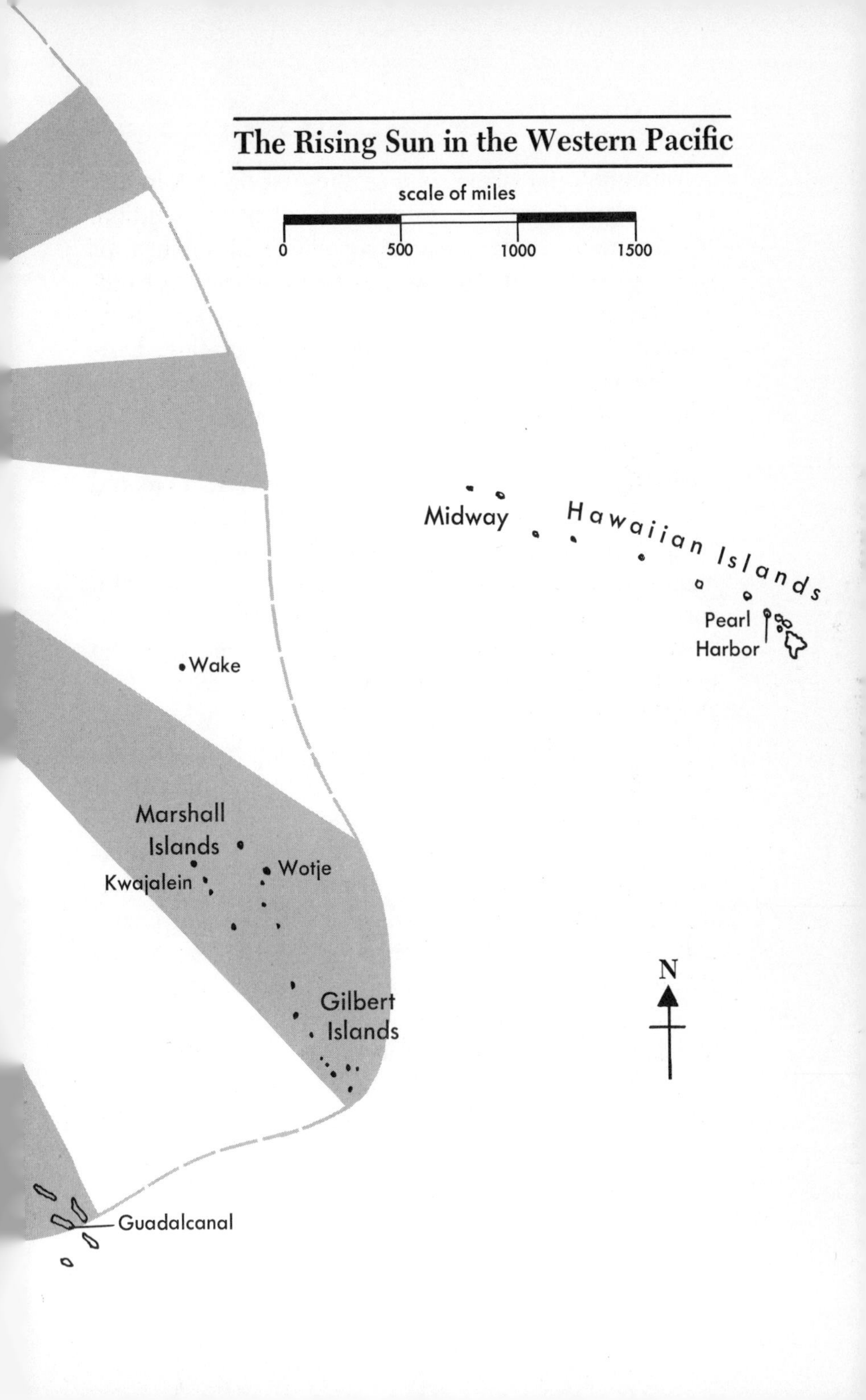

The Rising Sun in the Western Pacific

scale of miles

0   500   1000   1500

Midway Hawaiian Islands

Pearl
Harbor

• Wake

Marshall
Islands
Kwajalein • Wotje

Gilbert
Islands

N

• Guadalcanal

Yamamoto had been one of the first officers in any navy to appreciate the importance of naval aviation. As a captain, he was executive officer of Japan's air training command. He learned to fly when most officers his age refused to set foot in the rickety little aircraft the Japanese Navy then was operating. During the 1930s he played an important part in the development of Japan's aircraft industry, and later he influenced the Navy to build more aircraft carriers instead of concentrating only on battleships. In 1940 and 1941, as Commander in Chief, he put the Combined Fleet through a series of demanding maneuvers designed to improve gunnery, bombing marksmanship, torpedo bombing tactics, and night operations.

When he was sure that war would come soon, he convinced his government that it could be won only if the U.S. Pacific Fleet were destroyed quickly by a surprise attack. Isoroku Yamamoto, who had tried to avoid World War II, was the architect and planner of the Japanese attack on Pearl Harbor.

In the seventeen days after the Pearl Harbor attack, Japanese troops landed at nine points in the Philippines, on the American islands of Wake and Guam in the central Pacific, at three points on the Malay Peninsula, on the Dutch island of Borneo, and at the British crown colony of Hong Kong. The kingdom of Thailand, invaded from Indochina, surrendered on December 9. The following day, the British battleships *Prince of Wales* and *Repulse* were sunk by land-based planes near Singapore.

The United States, Great Britain, and the Netherlands fought back as best they could. American destroyers sank four Japanese troop transports in January. But most of the news that month, and in February and March, too, was bad. The cruiser *Marblehead* was badly mauled on February 4, north of Bali, and had to return to the United States for repairs. The British garrison at Singapore surrendered on February 15. On the 27th, a British cruiser was heavily damaged, while two British destroyers, two Dutch cruisers, and a Dutch destroyer were sunk in the Java Sea. Two more cruisers, one British and one American, were sunk by units of Yamamoto's Combined Fleet near Java on March 1. By the middle of March, Japan controlled several million square miles of land and sea from Tokyo east to a line running through Wake, the Marshall Islands, and the Gilberts. The southern boundary of Japan's new empire ran through Rabaul, across the top of New Guinea, and south of Java and Sumatra.

In April, four months after Pearl Harbor, the United States struck back. The U.S. Navy had no long-range bombers, and the Army Air Corps had no advance bases, but working together the two services mounted an attack on Tokyo itself. Sixteen Army B-25 bombers were loaded aboard the carrier *Hornet* at San Francisco and ferried to within 700 miles of Japan. Then the big planes took off for Tokyo, under the command of Lieutenant Colonel James Doolittle. Thirteen attacked the Japanese capital, while the other three hit smaller industrial cities. Doolittle and his fliers, unable to land their land planes on the carrier again, flew on to China.

The attack caused little real damage, but it shook the Japanese high command. Yamamoto was particularly disturbed. As Commander in Chief of the Combined Fleet, he was personally responsible for protecting the Emperor and the home islands from attack from the sea. His carrier planes had sunk plenty of battleships at Pearl Harbor, but they had failed to find the American carriers, which were at sea. Now he insisted again on the strategy he had been preaching for months. The American carriers must be destroyed, and destroyed soon.

Yamamoto's decision to engage the American carriers brought about the Battle of Midway.

Val

3.

Yamamoto's Plan

Admiral Yamamoto knew that Nimitz would want to put off a major engagement until he had had time to rebuild the U.S. Pacific Fleet. American industry was just beginning to build up to a wartime peak. Soon ships and planes would be pouring out of building yards and factories. Meanwhile, Nimitz needed time.

Time was just what Yamamoto could not afford. He needed to fight a major battle now, before the Pacific Fleet could regain its strength.

Midway was the bait with which Yamamoto hoped to lure Nimitz into that decisive battle. He knew that Nimitz needed to hold Midway. He was sure that if Midway were attacked Nimitz would send his fleet out to fight.

In March and April, even before the Doolittle raid, Yamamoto had been arguing with his superiors in Tokyo, urging them to approve his plan for an early attack on Midway. Doolittle's bombs settled the argument. The Midway attack was set for the first week of June 1942.

Yamamoto expected that most ships of the U.S. Pacific Fleet would be at Pearl Harbor. He planned two thrusts to lure them out for the fight. First he would attack the Aleutians, the chain of American islands that runs westward across the northern Pacific from the southwest corner of Alaska. Since an attack on these islands could mean that the Japanese were about to attack Alaska itself, Yamamoto believed that an attack there would entice the American carriers out into the open sea.

The next day, planes from a second and much larger Japanese force would bomb and strafe Midway. Two mornings later, Japanese troops would land on Sand Island and Eastern Island.

Yamamoto expected that Midway would fall quickly. Then the huge Japanese naval force which had been supporting the invasion would be free to attack the American fleet.

Yamamoto expected that Nimitz would send his carriers north to repel the Aleutian attack. This would take them out of position to protect Midway. Yamamoto believed that the Americans would head south again just as soon as Nimitz realized that the real fight was to be at Midway. But by that time Midway should have fallen, and Yamamoto's carriers would be ready and waiting. He hoped to surprise the American carriers at sea, somewhere between Midway and the Aleutians. In a battle between carrier forces, the Japanese would have the advantage of numbers as well as surprise, and Yamamoto expected to inflict heavy damage on the American flat-tops. Then his battle-ships, which would be lurking about a half-day's steaming behind the carriers, would rush in and fin-ish off the crippled American ships with their big guns.

Yamamoto believed that Nimitz might have two— or at most three—large aircraft carriers at Pearl Harbor, plus perhaps another two or three small car-riers. He expected that they would be supported by two battleships, about a dozen cruisers, and about 30 destroyers. Against this force the Japanese admiral planned to pit four first-line carriers, four smaller car-riers, 11 battleships, and more than 80 cruisers and destroyers. And Yamamoto thought his estimate of Nimitz's strength might be high, for the Japanese be-lieved that they had sunk two American carriers on May 8 in the Battle of the Coral Sea.

The estimate *was* high. Nimitz had no small car-riers at Pearl, and no battleships fast enough to steam with a carrier task force. Also, Yamamoto greatly overestimated American cruiser and destroyer strength. But only one American carrier had gone down in the Battle of the Coral Sea.

That two-day engagement was the first major battle in which aircraft carried out all the attacks, and op-posing surface ships never came within sight of each other. Planes from the American carriers *Lexington* and *Yorktown* sank a Japanese light carrier, damaged a large carrier, and shot down a good many planes from a second large flat-top. *Lexington* was sunk.

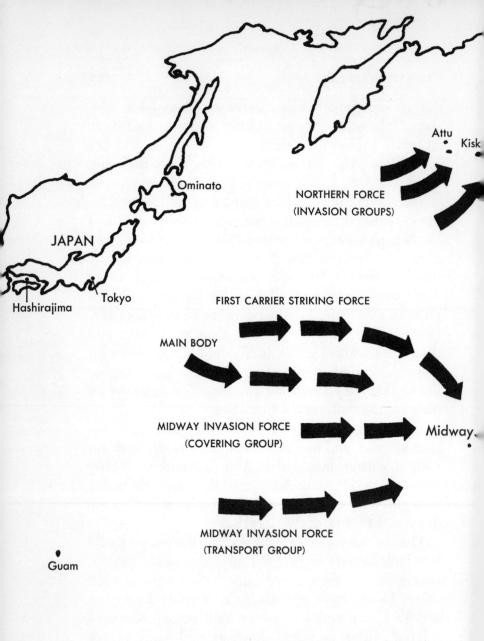

Ominato

Attu   Kisk

NORTHERN FORCE
(INVASION GROUPS)

JAPAN

Tokyo

Hashirajima

FIRST CARRIER STRIKING FORCE

MAIN BODY

MIDWAY INVASION FORCE
(COVERING GROUP)

Midway

MIDWAY INVASION FORCE
(TRANSPORT GROUP)

Guam

Marshall Islands

Kwajalein   Wotje

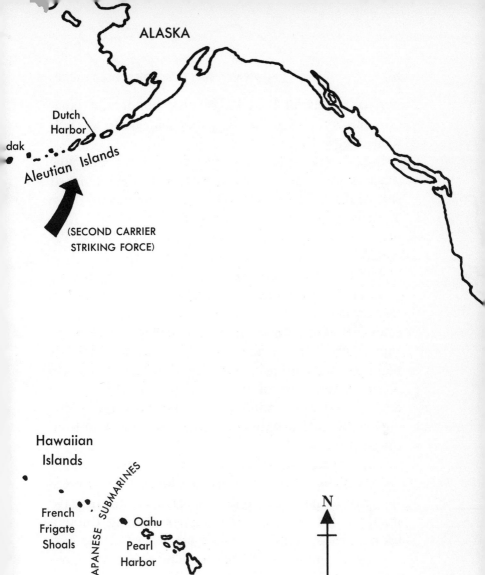

ALASKA

Dutch
Harbor

dak

Aleutian Islands

(SECOND CARRIER
STRIKING FORCE)

Hawaiian
Islands

French
Frigate
Shoals

JAPANESE SUBMARINES

Oahu

Pearl
Harbor

N

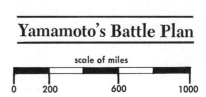

Yamamoto's Battle Plan

scale of miles

0   200   600   1000

Yorktown was hit by a large aerial bomb, and Japanese pilots reported that they had sent her to the bottom, along with *Lexington*.

But *Yorktown* had survived the battle, and now she was steaming toward Pearl Harbor for repairs. If she could be repaired in time, Nimitz would have three large carriers, *Yorktown*, *Enterprise*, and *Hornet*. But even if *Yorktown* took part in the battle, Yamamoto would have by far the superior fleet.

And Yamamoto was counting heavily on surprise.

To surprise the enemy, however, it is necessary to know where he is, and Yamamoto had no really good source of information on American fleet movements. Japan's pre-war spy network in the Hawaiian Islands had been broken up by American intelligence officers within a few days of the Pearl Harbor attack. This left the Japanese admiral with no eyes inside the enemy camp. The only alternative was to look in from the outside.

There were a number of ways in which he might do this. Yamamoto considered sending a submarine to snoop near the entrance to Pearl Harbor, but he gave up that idea. A submarine skipper, looking through his periscope, could see only a small part of the harbor. He could not send back the kind of report Yamamoto needed. To send back any kind of report, in fact, he would have to take his boat into dangerously shallow water and risk being attacked by American planes or patrol craft.

The best way of counting ships at Pearl Harbor

would be from the air. Some of Japan's larger submarines carried tiny seaplanes in watertight hangars on their decks. A few of these planes might be launched a hundred miles or more from Pearl Harbor and recovered later by their mother ships. But this, too, looked risky. The little planes were slow and carried very little armament. Hawaiian air defenses had been improved considerably since December 7, and it seemed unlikely that the little seaplanes would survive such a mission.

This left the Japanese Navy's huge Kawanishi seaplanes, which were available in 1942 only because Yamamoto himself had sponsored their development in the 1930s. Pearl Harbor was just out of range from the Japanese seaplane base at Wotje in the Marshall Islands, but the big, four-engine planes could get to Pearl and back if they could make one stop on the way for fuel. In March two of these flying boats had flown from Wotje to French Frigate Shoals, an uninhabited atoll 500 miles northwest of Hawaii, refueled there from a submarine, and made a night reconnaissance over Pearl Harbor, returning safely to Wotje nonstop. The flight was nicknamed "Operation K," for Kawanishi.

Yamamoto decided to repeat Operation K between May 31 and June 3. This should give him an accurate count of the American ships in Pearl Harbor.

He also ordered three submarine patrols established northwest of Hawaii, where they would detect —and might be able to sink—any carriers heading for either Midway or the Aleutians. The submarines were to be on station by June 3.

The attack on the Aleutians would begin that day. Carriers would strike Midway on June 4. Troops would begin landing in the Aleutians the morning of the fifth. That night, troop transports would approach Midway by moonlight. Japanese soldiers would pour ashore in landing barges at dawn on June 6 to capture Midway's two little islands. Then the Japanese Fleet would be free to attack the American carriers, which should be approaching from the northeast, after making a futile run north to protect the Aleutians.

A major sea battle should take place on June 6 or 7. By the morning of June 8, Yamamoto should be master of the Pacific.

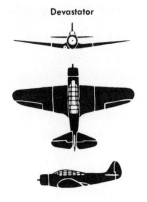
Devastator

4.

Nimitz Prepares for Battle

In Washington and at Pearl Harbor, American intelligence officers were trying to predict Yamamoto's next move. Unknown to Yamamoto, the Americans had broken some of Japan's secret naval codes. This meant that the intelligence section of Nimitz's staff could intercept and decipher many of the Japanese Navy's most secret messages.

Even when they could not understand the messages themselves, these officers could get information just by studying the patterns of Japanese radio traffic. During April, for instance, they noticed that the Commander in Chief of the Japanese Combined Fleet and his major subordinate commanders were sending many more messages than usual, and that they were addressing a very large number and variety of ships. From this information alone, they could guess that Yamamoto was planning a large operation.

Nimitz believed that this operation would be an attack on Midway. He could not be sure of this, however, for the Japanese always referred to their objective by the code letters "AF." Nimitz believed that "AF" was Midway, but it could be Oahu. Perhaps Yamamoto was planning another strike on Pearl Harbor, to be followed by an invasion of the Hawaiian Islands.

The problem was solved by Commander Joseph Rochefort, an intelligence officer on Nimitz's staff at Pearl Harbor. He instructed Captain Simard at Midway to send a radio message in plain English—not encoded—reporting that his water-distilling plant had broken down. Rochefort knew that the Japanese would be listening.

The message was sent, and Nimitz's staff waited hopefully. They did not have long to wait. In a few days they intercepted and decoded a Japanese message announcing that "AF" was short of water. Nimitz had been right. Yamamoto's target was Midway.

American intelligence officers also read enough Japanese messages to guess that the attack on the Aleutians was intended to draw the Pacific Fleet away from the main action. Knowing this, Nimitz ordered Rear Admiral Robert Theobald to take only a small task force of cruisers, destroyers, submarines, and land-based aircraft to Alaska. Meanwhile Nimitz kept most of his strength in the central Pacific to protect Midway and engage the Japanese fleet.

Nimitz planned his defense of Midway around his three aircraft carriers, *Yorktown*, *Enterprise*, and *Hornet*.

Traditionally, every navy in the world had considered its battleships to be its most important weapons. These heavily armored dreadnoughts carried 16-inch guns which could fire armor-piercing shells each weighing a ton a distance of more than 20 miles. They also carried smaller guns for close-in fighting, anti-aircraft guns, and small scout seaplanes which were launched by catapult and hoisted back aboard after landing on the sea.

The growth of naval aviation changed all this, and the Japanese attack on Pearl Harbor proved, if anyone still doubted it, that the aircraft carrier was the major fighting ship of the future. By 1942 the aircraft carrier had become the most important ship in both the Japanese and the American fleets.

An aircraft carrier is a floating air base, complete with landing field, control tower, repair shops, storage tanks for aviation fuel, and magazines for storing aerial bombs and torpedoes. It also has offices, a hospital, mess halls, and living space for the aviators, the ship's officers, and the sailors who keep the ship going and keep the planes in flying condition.

Yorktown, *Enterprise*, and *Hornet* were "sister ships," which means that they were nearly identical, having been built from almost the same plans. *Enterprise* and *Yorktown* were begun in 1934 and commissioned in 1938. *Hornet*'s keel was laid in 1939. Because of the outbreak of war in Europe and the growing danger of war in the Pacific, her construction was speeded up. She joined the fleet in 1941. All three ships were about 770 feet long at the water line and about 85 feet wide.

Enterprise photographed (in 1944) from an SBD Dauntless dive bomber which has just taken off. Another SBD is making its take-off run down the flight deck.

A carrier's main deck, three levels above the water line, was arranged as one huge hangar space for storing and repairing airplanes. Above the hangar deck was the flight deck, a long, flat runway from which the first American carriers got their nickname, "flattop." The flight deck usually extended just a bit farther fore and aft than the hull of the ship. The overall length of each of these three carriers was exactly 809½ feet. (By comparison, a football field is only 300 feet long.)

To avoid obstructing the flight deck, the ship's superstructure—called the "island"—was placed at one side. The island contained the smokestack, the captain's navigation bridge, the admiral's flag bridge, and "pri-fly," the primary flight-control station. In

American carriers this island was always on the right side of the ship facing the bow—that is, the starboard side. On most Japanese carriers the island also was to starboard, but a few were built with the island on the port (left) side. In both Japanese and American carriers, planes were moved from hangar deck to flight deck on huge elevators, one near the bow and a second slightly aft of the island. Some carriers had three elevators, one forward, one aft, and one amidships.

Enterprise, Hornet, and *Yorktown* were each taller than a 12-story building from keel to bridge. They could steam at more than 30 knots. (The term "knot" means "nautical mile per hour." A nautical mile is a little longer than a statute mile, which is the mile

An SBD rises on the elevator from the hangar deck to the flight deck of the carrier *Enterprise.*

measure used on land. Seven nautical miles equal approximately eight statute miles.)

Each ship carried from 75 to 80 planes—a mixed load of fighters, dive bombers (which also were used as scouts), and torpedo planes. The crew of each carrier, including the air group, numbered more than 2000 officers and men.

Today's aircraft carriers are nearly half again as large as the ships of World War II and carry as many as 4000 officers and men. Their jet planes, flying faster than the speed of sound, are larger, have a much longer range, and can carry a more powerful payload than ever was dreamed of in World War II. But in 1942 ships like *Yorktown*, *Hornet*, and *Enterprise*, and the Japanese carriers *Kaga* and *Akagi*, were the most powerful fighting ships afloat.

Some of the fighter planes of the carrier's air group always flew into battle with the dive bombers and torpedo planes to protect them from enemy fighters. Others were kept near the task force to protect the carrier against attack by enemy dive bombers and torpedo planes. The fighters that stayed behind to protect the carrier were called the Combat Air Patrol —CAP for short.

In addition to their CAP, *Yorktown*, *Hornet*, and *Enterprise* were protected by eight 5-inch dual-purpose guns apiece. These guns could be used against either aircraft or surface targets. Each ship also carried more than 30 smaller machine guns intended chiefly for anti-aircraft protection.

Anti-aircraft guns along the starboard side of *Yorktown*, just forward of the island. Starting in the foreground: a single 20-mm mount with two flak shields; one quad-mount 40-mm gun; five more single 20-mm mounts; two 5-inch dual-purpose guns.

An aircraft carrier was too important a ship and too tempting a target to trust its safety entirely to its own fighter planes and these few guns. Each carrier was assigned one or two cruisers and several destroyers for additional protection. Cruisers mounted 6-inch or 8-inch guns for use against enemy ships or other surface targets. They also had several 5-inch dual-purpose guns and smaller anti-aircraft guns like those on the carriers.

Destroyers are smaller than cruisers, and faster. During World War II they mounted 5-inch dual-purpose guns, smaller anti-aircraft guns, and torpedoes. They also carried depth charges for use against submarines.

Admiral Nimitz had eight cruisers and 15 destroyers to protect his three carriers. They added 64 8-inch guns, 142 5-inchers, and more than twice that number of smaller anti-aircraft guns to the defensive armament of the task force.

Like Yamamoto, Admiral Nimitz did not have an accurate estimate of his enemy's strength. He expected the Japanese fleet to include four or five carriers against his three; 12 to 14 cruisers against his eight; 16 to 24 destroyers against his 15; and at least 25 submarines to his 19. He also expected the enemy to have from two to four fast battleships. The nearest seaworthy American battle wagons were off San Francisco, and they were much too old and slow to operate with the fast carriers.

Unlike Admiral Yamamoto, who guessed high, Nimitz underestimated the size of the enemy fleet. (The Japanese and American forces are listed in the Appendix.)

Nimitz planned to send his fleet to sea several days before the Japanese attack. They would be waiting near Midway. When Yamamoto attacked, Nimitz's captains might find themselves badly outnumbered, but at least they would not be surprised.

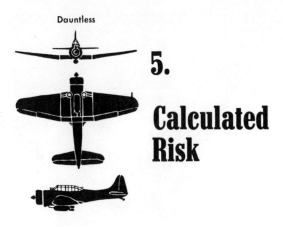
Dauntless

5.

Calculated Risk

Yamamoto's carriers got under way for the Battle of Midway the morning of May 27, 1942. To Admiral Yamamoto, the occasion must have been filled with emotion. The scene was Hashirajima, a naval base on the Inland Sea near Etajima, the Japanese naval academy. The day was Navy Day, a holiday commemorating the great Japanese victory in Tsushima Strait, the victory that gave young Ensign Yamamoto his first taste of the glory and pain of battle.

From the bridge of his flagship, the huge battleship *Yamato*, Yamamoto watched with approval as the carrier *Akagi* hoisted the red-and-white naval ensign, bearing the symbol of the rising sun, and then raised signal flags ordering the carrier force to sortie from the anchorage. The first ships to weigh anchor were the destroyers of Rear Admiral Susumu Kimura's Screening Group. Next came Rear Admiral Hiroake Abe's Support Group, the cruisers *Tone* and *Chikuma* and battleships *Haruna* and *Kirishima*. Behind the battle wagons came the aircraft carriers,

Vice Admiral Chuichi Nagumo, commander of the First Carrier Striking Force.

Akagi and *Kaga* (a pair of giants to match *Enterprise, Yorktown,* and *Hornet*) and the carriers *Hiryu* and *Soryu* (only slightly smaller).

From *Akagi*'s mast flew the three-star flag of Vice Admiral Chuichi Nagumo. Nagumo was not an aviator, but he had commanded the force of six carriers that attacked Pearl Harbor, and he had since led carrier strikes in the South Pacific and the Indian Ocean. He was an experienced officer, respected by his juniors and seniors. He was the obvious choice to command Yamamoto's carriers in the Battle of Midway. As Commander Carrier Division One, Nagumo would retain immediate tactical command of *Akagi* and *Kaga*, the two ships of his division. At the same time, he also would command the entire Carrier Striking Force of four carriers and its protective screen—26 ships in all.

Rear Admiral Tamon Yamaguchi flew his flag in *Hiryu*. As Commander Carrier Division Two, he commanded the carriers *Hiryu* and *Soryu*.

Steaming in single file, at half-mile intervals, the ships of Vice Admiral Nagumo's imposing Carrier Striking Force sailed out of the Inland Sea and into the Pacific. Once in the open sea, the armada shifted into a wartime steaming formation. The four carriers formed two columns, Nagumo's division to starboard, Yamaguchi's to port. Forward of the carriers came the cruisers *Tone* and *Chikuma*. The battleships *Haruna* and *Kirishima* brought up the rear. Surrounding the "heavies" were the eleven destroyers of Kimura's Screening Group, led by the sleek light cruiser *Nagara*.

Once at sea, the ships of the Carrier Striking Force turned off their radio transmitters, except for the high-frequency sets used to talk from ship to ship. Very high frequency (VHF) radio waves travel in a straight line, like light. This limits their range to a line-of-sight from the transmitter, for when the waves reach the horizon, they continue in a straight line into the sky and are lost forever. This fact makes it possible to use VHF radio between the ships of a naval formation without danger of being overheard by an enemy on the surface many miles away. But a task force at sea cannot use its long-range ship-to-shore radio without risk of being overheard by the enemy and thus giving away its position.

This fact may account for Yamamoto's failure to

send Nagumo one piece of bad news. For the Japanese submarines which he had sent to French Frigate Shoals to refuel his reconnaissance seaplanes found, when they arrived, that an American seaplane tender was anchored in the lagoon. American seaplanes apparently were using the Shoals as a temporary base. The submarines relayed this information to Kwajalein, Operation K was canceled, and this was reported to the Commander in Chief.

But neither Admiral Yamamoto nor the submarine commander at Kwajalein nor Naval Headquarters at Tokyo—where all communications were monitored— notified Nagumo that the reconnaissance plan had been canceled. There was no alternate plan, and no Japanese commander ordered any intelligence-gathering operation to take its place.

While the Japanese fleet steamed out of the Inland Sea toward Midway, USS *Yorktown* limped into Pearl Harbor. During the Battle of the Coral Sea 19 days earlier, her air group had lost a good many planes and pilots. *Yorktown* had successfully dodged nine torpedoes, but one 800-pound bomb had penetrated her flight deck, just inboard of the island, exploding below the hangar deck. The explosion and the fire that followed it had damaged bulkheads, watertight doors, machinery, and electrical cables. *Yorktown* steamed home under her own power, but repair officers estimated that it would take about three months to put the carrier back into first-class fighting trim.

Admiral Nimitz could not wait three months. He had a war to fight, and he expected to need *Yorktown* in less than a week. He ordered the Pearl Harbor Navy Yard to make temporary repairs and to get the ship ready for sea as soon as possible.

In a matter of hours *Yorktown* was resting on huge wooden blocks in a dry dock, and repair crews were swarming over her battered hull. Damaged bulkheads were repaired or shored up with heavy timbers. Machinery was put back into working order. Burned electrical cables were replaced. Pipe fitters repaired steam and fuel lines and aviation gasoline lines which

Yorktown in dry dock at Pearl Harbor just before the Battle of Midway. Shipyard cranes hoisted some of the small railroad cars (at left) directly to the flight deck for unloading.

had been damaged by the Japanese bomb. It was not possible, of course, to repair the ship completely. Many formerly watertight doors and hatches were badly sprung and could not be refitted in so short a time. Three of *Yorktown*'s nine boilers were not fully repaired. But the yard workers did all they could. The carrier's supply lockers were also refilled. To save time, whole railroad cars were hoisted aboard her flight deck by the giant shipyard cranes and unloaded by crewmen. The stores were piled on the deck elevators and then taken below.

The Navy Yard crews worked around the clock. In less than two days, the carrier was afloat again with steam in her boilers. Three of her air group's four squadrons were replaced with units which had been waiting in Hawaii for another carrier then being repaired on the west coast. When *Yorktown* sailed from Pearl Harbor the morning of May 30, she may not have been quite like new; but she was ready to take her place in the fleet until time could be found for a more thorough overhaul.

In contrast, it was two months before the Japanese carrier *Shokaku*, which also had been damaged in the Battle of the Coral Sea, was ready for sea again. And *Shokaku*'s sister ship, *Zuikaku*, missed the Battle of Midway because the Japanese Navy could not replace the airmen and planes she had lost in the Coral Sea quickly enough for her to join Nagumo's Carrier Striking Force.

While *Yorktown* was still in dry dock, Task Force

Rear Admiral Raymond A. Spruance, commander of Task Force 16 at Midway (left), and Rear Admiral Frank Jack Fletcher, commander of Task Force 17 at Midway. (Both were later promoted to the rank of four-star admiral.)

16, built around the carriers *Enterprise* and *Hornet*, sailed from Pearl Harbor. The two-star flag of Rear Admiral Raymond A. Spruance flew in *Enterprise*. As task-force commander, Spruance issued tactical orders directly to the commanding officers of the two carriers, as well as to Rear Admiral Thomas C. Kinkaid, commander of the cruiser and destroyer escorts. The admiral's orders were passed from the flag bridge—an area in *Enterprise*'s island set aside for the use of the admiral and his staff—to Captain George D. Murray, commanding officer of *Enterprise*, by telephone. The admiral's orders went to *Hornet* and the escort task groups by signal flag, short-range radio, or flashing light.

Following Nimitz's orders, Spruance sailed his task force to a point 350 miles northeast of Midway, timing his arrival to rendezvous there with Task Force

17, the *Yorktown* group. Since Rear Admiral Frank Jack Fletcher, commander of Task Force 17, was senior to Spruance, Fletcher assumed command. Spruance, however, retained immediate tactical control of Task Force 16, subject to general instructions from Fletcher.

Admiral Nimitz exercised broad command over the task forces of Fletcher and Spruance, Captain Simard's forces on Midway, Rear Admiral Theobald's Task Force 8 in the Aleutians, and Rear Admiral English's submarine force. Unlike Admiral Yamamoto, who flew his flag in the battleship *Yamato*, operating with the Main Body of the Combined Fleet, Nimitz remained ashore. This gave him the advantage of superior communications, for he had excellent cable connections between his Pearl Harbor headquarters and Midway to the west and Washington to the east. He could also use his shore-based radio freely to broadcast instructions to the fleet. Yamamoto, on the other hand, could not use his long-range radio without risk of being overheard. If he transmitted for any length of time, Nimitz's forces could locate his flagship accurately with radio direction finders, thus completely robbing him of his supposed advantage of surprise.

Admiral Nimitz's battle order referred to the rendezvous point by a code name, "Point Luck." The name was well chosen, for in challenging the huge Japanese fleet Fletcher and Spruance would need all the luck they could get.

Nimitz had cautioned the two rear admirals to expose their ships to attack by superior forces only if they believed they could inflict greater damage on the enemy than they themselves might suffer. "You will be governed," he ordered, "by the principle of calculated risk."

Fletcher and Spruance steamed together the night of June 2, waiting for that moment of risk. Some luck was already with them, for in order to meet at Point Luck that day, both task forces had to steam through the areas in which the Japanese submarine patrols were to be established. But the American task forces passed these areas several days before the Japanese subs could reach their station. Thus neither Operation K, which was canceled, nor the submarine patrols, which were established too late, gave Yamamoto any warning that the American ships had put to sea.

Meanwhile, less than a thousand miles west of Midway, Vice Admiral Kondo's Midway Invasion Force was steaming directly toward the atoll. Several hundred miles north of Kondo's transports, hidden by thick clouds, Vice Admiral Nagumo's Carrier Striking Force also was steaming eastward. Admiral Yamamoto, with his Main Body of battleships and cruisers, was about 600 miles west of the carriers. And far to the north, under cover of a heavy fog, Vice Admiral Moshiro Hosogaya's Northern Force was moving into position for its attack on the Aleutians.

It was in the Aleutians that the Battle of Midway was about to begin.

Zero

6.

Action in the North

Vice Admiral Hosogaya's Northern Force had sailed from the port of Ominato in northern Japan the morning of May 26. The force consisted of Rear Admiral Kakuji Kakuta's Second Carrier Striking Force and two small invasion forces.

Kakuta's carrier group was built around two small flat-tops, *Ryujo* and *Junyo*. Between them, the two ships carried less than 90 planes. They were escorted by two heavy cruisers and three destroyers. The invasion troops, which were carried in three transports, consisted of 1200 soldiers, 550 men of the Special Naval Landing Force, and 700 labor troops with heavy construction equipment. The invasion forces also were escorted by cruisers and destroyers.

Kakuta's mission was to launch air strikes against American bases in the Aleutians. Then the two landing forces would separate. One would seize the islands of Adak and Attu. The other would occupy Kiska.

Weather in the northern Pacific seldom is pleasant. A current of warm water, called the Japan Current, flows northward from the Philippines, passes east of Japan, and then crosses the northern Pacific to Alaska. As it approaches the Aleutians, the warm water meets cold air which has drifted down from the Arctic. The result is the same as when a pan of warm water is placed in the freezing compartment of a refrigerator. The water gets cold, and steam rises into the air. On a larger scale, the combination of warm water and cold air in the northern Pacific causes low fog and a heavy layer of higher clouds. This combination results in some of the worst flying weather in the world.

The Northern Force found itself in a dense fog before nightfall. This was not unexpected, and Admiral Hosogaya looked at the fog as a mixed blessing. It would make navigation a bit difficult, but it also would hide his ships from the prying eyes of American submarine skippers and American patrol pilots. Hosogaya's force would have to steam slowly, since none of the ships were equipped with radar. But they had plenty of time.

Kakuta's carriers were in striking position the morning of June 3. They were north of the 50th parallel and about 180 miles from Dutch Harbor, the most important United States base in the Aleutians. It was time to attack.

The Japanese knew very little about Dutch Harbor. Their maps were more than 30 years old, and in many places the shorelines had been drawn almost entirely on the basis of guesswork. They had only one photograph of the target area. It, too, was old. Japanese intelligence officers believed that Dutch Harbor was protected by a U.S. Army division, and that Kiska and Attu also were fortified. Actually, there were fewer than 6000 soldiers, sailors, and Marines at Dutch Harbor, and only ten unarmed weather observers at Kiska. The only Americans on Attu were a pair of missionaries.

Summer nights are short in the northern latitudes. The sun rose over Kakuta's Second Carrier Striking Force at 2:58 the morning of June 3. Fifteen minutes earlier, the faint light of the coming dawn had begun to penetrate the dense fog surrounding the ships. On *Ryujo*'s bridge, fur-clad officers, straining their eyes into the distance, finally could see the dim outline of *Junyo*, barely a mile and a half away. At last it was light enough to launch aircraft. Admiral Kakuta nodded toward his signal officer. *Ryujo*'s blinker lights flashed the word:

SQUADRONS TAKE OFF FOR ATTACK.

Fighters and bombers already were warming their engines on the flight decks of both carriers. The temperature was below freezing, and no pilot wanted a cold engine that might lose power just as he soared over the bow of the ship. The Japanese Navy had not been trained for cold-weather operations, and Kakuta's pilots were none too happy with this Aleutian assignment. Navigation would be a problem. Visibility was terrible. The pilot who missed his target might fly into the side of a mountain, invisible behind the clouds. The pilot who missed his carrier when he returned from the mission almost certainly would freeze to death in the icy sea.

Engines roared. Planes rolled forward, picked up speed, and disappeared into the fog. Kakuta launched only 35 planes—11 bombers and six fighters from *Ryujo*, 12 bombers and a half-dozen fighters from *Junyo*. One of *Ryujo*'s bombers crashed into the sea on take-off, but an alert destroyer skipper moved his ship in quickly to rescue the crew.

With such poor visibility and a ceiling of only about 500 feet, it was impossible for the planes to fly in formation. Instead, they straggled almost independently toward the target. *Junyo*'s planes never did find Dutch Harbor. They shot down an American seaplane, which they met quite by accident en route, but finally they had to return to their carrier without dropping a bomb. Only nine bombers and three fighters from *Ryujo* actually found Dutch Harbor. These 12 pilots were lucky enough to come on a break in the clouds through which they could see the American base. They attacked and managed to set fire to some fuel tanks, shoot up a seaplane moored in the bay, and damage a number of buildings. About 25 Americans were killed in the attack, which lasted about 20 minutes.

One Japanese fighter plane was hit by American anti-aircraft fire. It crash-landed on an island 20 miles away. The pilot was killed, but the plane was not badly damaged. Five weeks later an American search

Buildings burning fiercely at Dutch Harbor after the Japanese attack.

party found the plane. It was the first Japanese Zero to fall into American hands. This one plane yielded so much valuable information to American intelligence officers that its loss far outweighed all the damage the Japanese had inflicted on Dutch Harbor.

On their way back to *Ryujo* the remaining 11 pilots passed over Makushin Bay on the coast of Unalaska Island. There they spotted several American destroyers at anchor. This news was radioed back to Admiral Kakuta, who immediately ordered his two carriers to launch the rest of their aircraft and attack the ships. Even the small seaplanes of the cruiser escort were sent on this strike.

While this second wave of Japanese planes was in the air, the treacherous Aleutian weather closed in

American salvage party with the Zero that crashed in the Aleutians.

over Dutch Harbor and Makushin Bay. The attackers never found the destroyers, but two Japanese planes were shot down by Army Air Corps fighters flying from a new base at Otter Point, and two more were damaged. This was quite a surprise for the Japanese, who had no idea that the United States had another air base near Dutch Harbor.

Admiral Kakuta planned another attack for the next morning. This time the target was to be Adak. The mission was to soften up the island's defenses in preparation for invasion. The weather was so bad over Adak, however, that the planes could not find the target. Instead, they attacked Dutch Harbor again. The attackers—17 bombers and 15 fighters—had a profitable morning. Four newly built fuel tanks went up in flames. One wing of the base hospital was completely destroyed. An old merchant ship, which was being used as living quarters, was badly damaged. Bombs also destroyed part of a hangar which was still under construction. Eighteen Americans were killed.

Three more Japanese planes were shot down by Army Air Corps P-40 pursuit planes, but the Japanese losses were light compared to the damage their planes caused on the ground. In addition to the loss of men, buildings, and fuel tanks at Dutch Harbor, the attack cost the United States six seaplanes, two bombers, and a pair of fighters.

Admiral Theobald's Task Force 8 searched in vain for the Japanese carriers, but weather was on the enemy's side. The carriers were spotted only once, and attacked by Army Air Corps bombers. The high-flying planes scored no hits. Two were shot down in the attack.

A few days later, Hosogaya put his troops ashore at Kiska and Attu. Neither landing party met any resistance. The occupation of Adak was canceled, probably because that island was only 350 miles from the American air base at Otter Point.

The northern operation failed to pull the U.S. Pacific Fleet out of position, but it did end with Japanese troops on American soil. It was not very valuable soil —a pair of barren islands with a climate and terrain that made them nearly useless, either for construction of major bases or as stepping stones for invasion of

Japan or the United States. But with bases in the Aleutians, Japan had a northern anchor, of sorts, for its defense perimeter. In Yamamoto's master plan, the next point south in that defense line was Midway.

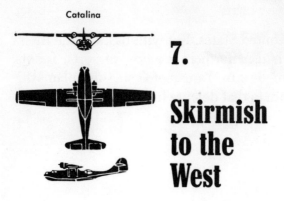
Catalina

7.

Skirmish to the West

While Kakuta's planes were attacking the fog-shrouded Aleutians, the other Japanese forces continued to converge on Midway.

Weather, always important in a war at sea, favored the attackers. The area to the northwest of Midway, beginning about 200 miles from the atoll, was covered with low clouds, fog, and occasional rain. This foul weather hid Vice Admiral Nagumo's Carrier Striking Force the morning of June 3. Farther south, Vice Admiral Kondo's Midway Invasion Force was just coming out of the bad weather. To the west, Yamamoto's Main Body still was hidden. Midway itself lay fully exposed under a cloudless sky.

Fletcher and Spruance were cruising northeast of Midway in clear weather, waiting for news.

More than 20 Midway-based patrol planes were searching the sea to the west. These planes were PBY-5 and PBY-5A Catalinas. The PBY-5 was a high-wing, twin-engine seaplane, 64 feet long, with a wingspan of 104 feet. It carried two pilots and seven or more crewmen. The PBY-5A was an amphibian version of the same plane. The PBY-5 could land only on water, while the 5A had retractable wheels and could land on water or on an airstrip ashore.

Both models cruised at 130 knots at 6000 feet, and could carry 4000 pounds of bombs or two torpedoes. Each was armed with four machine guns, two forward and two in turrets on either side of the fuselage, aft of the wing. Some of the newer planes were equipped with radar.

Captain Simard had 32 of the big patrol bombers at Midway. Beginning on May 30, 22 of them took off every morning before dawn, each one assigned to search a sector of the 700-mile-deep semicircle of lonely ocean to the northwest, west, and southwest of the atoll.

By the morning of June 3, Nagumo's carriers were within the range of the big patrol planes, but now luck was with the Japanese. Several times during the day American planes passed over the Carrier Striking Force, but none of these planes were equipped with radar. Men on the Japanese ships heard the aircraft engines, but the clouds were thick and the American pilots never saw the enemy carriers.

At nine o'clock that morning, however, the day stopped being routine. Ensign Jewell H. Reid, the pilot of one of Midway's PBY Catalinas, was almost at the end of his search. He had flown west for 700 miles, turned south, and was about to turn east again and head back to Midway. Suddenly, through a break in

Ensign Reid (perched up on aircraft) and the crew of his PBY Catalina, including a copilot, a navigator, a radioman, and aviation machinist's mates.

the clouds, Reid saw a large group of ships steaming eastward, toward Midway.

Staying beyond the range of anti-aircraft guns, Reid circled the formation. From his high altitude, it was impossible to identify the ships positively, but he counted about a dozen "heavies" steaming in two columns. Smaller ships, probably destroyers, were out ahead in a protective screen. Reid reported what he saw by radio, and then stayed with the enemy force for about two hours, continuing to report its movements.

From Reid's description, Captain Simard at Midway assumed that the force was Yamamoto's Main

Body. Obviously, it contained no carriers. If it had, Reid's slow-moving flying boat would have been shot down by fighter planes almost immediately. But from the size of the ships, their number, and their cruising formation, the big ones might be battleships and cruisers.

Simard ordered Lieutenant Colonel Walter Sweeney to take nine of his Army Air Corps B-17 bombers from Midway for an attack on the Japanese ships. The B-17s found the enemy at four that afternoon, approximately 600 miles west of Midway. Accustomed to bombing stationary targets ashore, the Air Corps fliers stayed high and released their bombs from the safe altitude of 10,000 feet. They were sure their reli-

B-17 Flying Fortresses

able Norden bombsights would put the bombs on target.

But the Norden bombsight had not been designed for moving targets. The Japanese saw the bombs coming. The ships broke formation and scattered, zigzagging as they went, and the bombs fell harmlessly into the sea.

The pilots, looking down from their lofty altitude, reported hits on two "battleships or heavy cruisers and two transports." Admiral English, commander of Nimitz's submarine force, promptly ordered USS *Cuttlefish* to leave her mid-Pacific patrol station and hunt down the four cripples. *Cuttlefish* did her best, but there were no cripples to be found. The pilots had mistaken the smoke and spray of near misses for hits. None of the Japanese ships was damaged even slightly by the B-17 attack.

Back at Pearl Harbor, Nimitz and his staff carefully analyzed the situation. From intercepted radio messages, they had a good idea of Yamamoto's strategy and the organization of his fleet. Nimitz was convinced that the carrier attack against Midway would come the next morning, probably from the northwest. The discovery of this group of large ships west of Midway fit the pattern. The group apparently did not contain carriers. The only conclusion was that the carriers were farther north, in which case the Main Body also should be north. The ships which Reid had found, and which the B-17s had attacked, must be the transports of Kondo's Invasion Force, still two days away from Midway, ready to steam in for the landing after the carriers had softened up Midway's defenses.

Aboard *Yorktown*, Rear Admiral Fletcher and his staff were coming to about the same conclusion when they received a coded radio message from Nimitz:

THAT IS NOT REPEAT NOT THE ENEMY STRIKING FORCE. IT IS THE LANDING FORCE. THE STRIKING FORCE WILL HIT FROM THE NORTHWEST AT DAYLIGHT TOMORROW.

The fact that Nimitz was able to send this message shows the wisdom of his decision to exercise command from headquarters ashore. Had he been at sea, like Yamamoto, he would have had to keep his conclusions to himself, hoping that Fletcher had made the same decision.

Whether the enemy ships Reid had found were battleships or transports, they were a threat to Captain Simard and Midway. Simard was determined to do whatever he could to sink them. He didn't have many weapons, but some of his PBY Catalinas had radar, and he was certain that the Japanese did not. The PBYs were slow, but if they attacked at night they had a good chance of scoring a hit.

Four radar-equipped Catalinas were armed that evening with aerial torpedoes. They took off after dark and flew westward, over the moonlit sea. The lead plane's radar picked up surface targets not long after midnight. A few minutes later, the pilots could see more than a dozen ships, clearly visible in the light of a nearly full moon. One by one the big, clumsy-looking "Cats" peeled off and made their low-level torpedo attacks. One "fish" hit. The explosion was impressive, and the pilots went home thinking that they, too, had disabled one of the enemy ships. But, like the Army Air Corps fliers, they were a bit too hopeful. The ship they hit was *Akebono Maru*, a tanker. Eleven men were killed and 13 wounded by the torpedo explosion, but the ship was slowed down for only a few minutes. She soon regained her place in the formation.

Rear Admiral Fletcher knew of the land-based air attacks on the Invasion Force, but he did not send any carrier planes to help. If he had, his planes would have been recognized and the Japanese would have known immediately that the American carriers were at sea. Instead, he heeded Nimitz's advice and observed "the principle of calculated risk." It would have been useful to sink the transports, but transports by themselves posed no threat to Midway. Troops could not land without protection from Nagumo's carriers, and it was carriers that Fletcher planned to sink. Japan could replace a dozen transports and 5000 soldiers, but carriers and carrier aircraft were another story. If Fletcher could sink the enemy carriers, he would win a major victory.

No, attacking the transports did not fit in with Nimitz's plan. Tonight Fletcher would wait. There would be plenty of inviting targets in the morning.

8.

Nagumo Strikes

Dawn was still an hour away. A faint glow had begun to appear in the east, just above the horizon. To the west the sky was brighter, lit by the moon. In every other direction both sea and sky were blue-black, seeming to run together without any horizon to divide them.

Occasionally a small wave would break on Midway's coral reef. Its shimmering white foam caught the moonlight for a moment and reflected it, making the narrow strip of gently churning water seem to glow with a cold fire. Then the fire would disappear, as quickly as it had come, and the outline of the atoll would be invisible again.

Overhead the stars danced, like a million tiny, flickering lights, far, far away, where the coming dawn had not yet touched the dome of the sky.

A warm, light breeze carried the faint smell of the sea to the Americans on Midway's islands, but not the smell of rain. There was not a cloud in the sky, and there was no hope that any would appear that day to hide Midway atoll. The men at Midway could expect a clear sky on June 4. If Nimitz was right, some time that day they could expect that sky to rain down fire and death.

In the cockpit of his PBY, Howard Ady pushed the throttle levers forward. The plane shook as its two engines began to race, their propellers biting into the warm tropic air. Slowly the clumsy-looking seaplane gathered speed. Soon its hull was partly out of the water—"on the step," its crew would say—as it skimmed across the surface of the lagoon. Lieutenant Ady pulled back on the control yoke. The big plane responded, rising a bit more, finally freeing itself from the water and climbing into the black sky.

Below, on Eastern Island's darkened air strip, Ady and his crew could see the blue-and-orange glow of exhaust flames where other planes were warming up. Then he was over the coral reef, still climbing. He banked and headed west. He had a long flight ahead of him—700 miles out and 700 miles back. He was not far on his way before the early dawn began to light up the sky above him and the sea below.

With the coming of daylight, Lieutenant Ady and his fellow PBY pilots began searching sea and sky. It was their job to find the Carrier Striking Force of Admiral Yamamoto's Combined Fleet.

Aboard the carrier *Yorktown* 200 miles to the north, Lieutenant Wallace Short, skipper of Scouting Squadron Five, was briefing his pilots. The enemy carriers were somewhere to the west. Japanese carrier planes might be taking off that very minute to attack Midway. Twenty or more long-range seaplanes and amphibians were searching the area from which that attack was expected to come. As an added precaution, Admiral Fletcher had ordered *Yorktown's* air group to make a 100-mile sweep north of the three American carriers, just in case the Japanese might be lurking close by.

Lieutenant Short finished his briefing. Ten pilots filed quietly out of the ready room and up the steep stairways—the Navy calls them "ladders"—leading to the darkened flight deck. In the dim glow of hooded red lights, the pilots found their planes, spotted at the after end of the flight deck, ready for take-off. A crewman, who would serve as radioman and gunner, was already at each plane.

At a signal from the ship's air officer, the pilots started their engines. The noise was deafening as the ten SBD Dauntless scout bombers warmed up. On the navigation bridge, high on the island, Captain Elliot Buckmaster, commanding officer of the carrier, gave the helmsman an order and the big carrier slowly turned into the wind. A few moments later, Buckmaster pressed down the "pri-fly" button on his intercom and gave a short, terse order:

"Launch 'em!"

The roar increased as engines turned up to take-off speed. Flight-deck crewmen, carefully avoiding the whirling propellers, crawled along the darkened deck

Captain Elliot Buckmaster, commanding officer of *Yorktown* in the battles of Coral Sea and Midway.

and pulled away the wheel chocks—blocks set under the wheels of each plane to keep it from moving with the wind or the motions of the ship. One by one the little planes roared down the narrow flight deck, over the bow, and into the darkness.

For a moment or two, Captain Buckmaster could see the dim blue flames of their exhausts against the sky. Then they faded from view, and there was nothing but black sky and black water, broken only by twinkling stars, the setting moon, and the faint glow of dawn in the east.

And 240 miles west of Midway, in the four carriers of Nagumo's Striking Force, more than a hundred pilots filed from their briefing rooms to their

planes. The weather was perfect. The sea was calm.
A slight headwind blew over the ships' bows. The carriers would not even have to change course to head
into the wind.

Pilots manned their planes. Engines sputtered, then
roared into life. One by one the pilots turned on their
red and blue running lights to signal that they were
ready for take-off. Soon the darkened decks were
spotted with colored lights, reflected by whirling
propellers.

On each carrier, the air officer swung a green lan-
tern in a wide circle over his head, the signal for flight
leaders to begin taking off. Suddenly, the four decks
were bathed by brilliant floodlights. Slowly at first,
their speed increasing as they roared down the long
flight decks, the lead planes took to the air. On deck,
crewmen cheered wildly as fighters, bombers, and
torpedo planes cleared the bows of the carriers and
flew toward the rising sun.

On the flag bridge of the carrier *Akagi*, Vice Admiral Nagumo watched the planes depart for Midway. Japanese records, published after the war, contain his estimate of the tactical situation that morning:

(1) The enemy fleet probably will come out to engage when the Midway landing operations are begun.

(2) Enemy air patrols from Midway will be heavier
to the south and westward, less heavy to the north
and northwest.

(3) The radius of enemy air patrols is estimated to
be approximately 500 miles.

(4) The enemy is not yet aware of our plan, and has not yet detected our task force.

(5) There is no evidence of an enemy task force in our vicinity.

(6) It is therefore possible for us to attack Midway, destroy land-based planes there, and support the landing operation. We can then turn around, meet an approaching enemy force and destroy it.

(7) Possible counterattacks by enemy land-based air surely can be repulsed by our interceptors and anti-aircraft fire.

Nagumo's first wave was made up of 108 planes. There were 36 Nakajima Type 97 torpedo bombers, called "Kates" by American intelligence officers. There were 36 Type 99 dive bombers, "Vals" to the Americans. And there were the same number of Mitsubishi Zero fighters. Lieutenant Joichi Tomonaga, commander of *Hiryu*'s air group, led the attack.

The 36 Kates, all from *Hiryu* and *Soryu*, were loaded with ordinary bombs instead of torpedoes, since their target was to be the base at Midway. Torpedoes are useful only against ships.

Kate was a single-engine plane with a cruising speed of about 145 knots. At that speed, it could attack a target about 450 nautical miles from its carrier and still have fuel enough to get back safely. It normally attacked at shorter ranges, however, to allow the pilot to fly faster while actually in battle, and to give him some "loiter time" over the target. Kate could carry one 1760-pound torpedo, slung below the fuselage, or bombs. It was flown by one pilot and carried one or two crewmen.

In addition to its bombs or torpedo, Kate was armed with three 7.7-millimeter machine guns. Two of the guns were fixed to fire forward. They were fired by the pilot and could be used to strafe targets on the ground as well as to fire at other planes. The third gun was operated by a crewman. It was carried on a flexible mount and could be aimed to either side of the plane. The bullets fired by 7.7-millimeter guns were slightly more than a quarter-inch in diameter—a bit larger than a .22-caliber rifle bullet but smaller than a .38-caliber slug.

Val also was a single-engine plane. It cruised a bit faster than Kate, normally at about 155 knots. Its range was about the same as Kate's, and it was armed with the same combination of machine guns. It carried only one crewman in addition to the pilot.

Val was fitted with two bomb racks under each wing, and carried about 800 pounds of bombs. Unlike Kate, which dropped its bombs or torpedo while flying level, Val was a dive bomber. Its attack began from an altitude of 12,000 feet or more. From that height, it would plunge down in a steep dive, dropping its bombs from an altitude of two to three thousand feet. The pilot might swoop on down to 500 feet or less before making his getaway almost "on the deck," where his plane would be a difficult target for shipboard guns or opposing fighter planes.

The Vals for Nagumo's strike against Midway

Val, the standard Japanese dive bomber, flew without retracting its landing gear. The heavy gear acted as a dive brake.

came from the carriers *Akagi* and *Kaga*.

The Mitsubishi Zero was just about the hottest fighter then in the sky. It was not as solidly built as the U.S. Navy's standard fighter, the F4F Wildcat. It could take a lot less punishment than most American fighters, but what it lacked in toughness it made up in performance. Its normal cruising speed was 210 knots, and it might dive on an enemy plane at almost twice that speed. In the first years of the war, the Zero could outclimb and outmaneuver every carrier plane the U.S. Navy had.

In addition to two 7.7-millimeter machine guns, it carried a pair of much harder-hitting 20-millimeter rapid-firing cannon which fired explosive shells. All its guns were fixed to fire forward, for the Zero was a single-seater and its guns were fired by the pilot.

The Zero's range, long for a fighter in those days, could be stretched to about 890 nautical miles by reducing cruising speed to 150 knots. By slowing down his Vals and Zeros to the cruising speed of the Kates, Lieutenant Tomonaga could expect to keep his 108-plane attack wave in formation during the roughly 200-mile flight to Midway. Once there, he planned to conduct a coordinated attack on the target, keeping his fighters over the atoll as long as the bombers needed protection. If he watched his speed and timing carefully, he should get his planes back to Nagumo's carriers with a few gallons of gas to spare.

Tomonaga's flight represented less than half of Nagumo's air strength. The admiral wisely kept a second wave of dive bombers, fighters, and torpedo planes on his carriers. He planned to mount a second assault on Midway if Tomonaga's attack failed to paralyze the island's defenders.

And just in case there should be any American ships in the neighborhood, Nagumo ordered the 36 Kates of his second wave armed with torpedoes instead of bombs. Nagumo's orders from Admiral Yamamoto were to destroy Midway's defenses, but also to sink American carriers. Nagumo did not believe there were any carriers nearby. But, if there were, he intended to be ready.

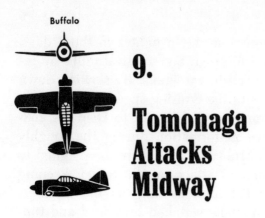

Buffalo

9.

Tomonaga Attacks Midway

At 5:30 A.M., as Lieutenant Tomonaga finished organizing his flight into a neat "V" formation and headed for Midway, Lieutenant Howard Ady's PBY broke through a hole in the clouds a few miles from Nagumo's carriers. Looking to his right, the pilot saw a white line on the surface of the sea. It could be only one thing, the wake of a fast-moving ship.

Ady brought his plane a bit lower and headed for the telltale wake. Soon there was a second streak. Then several more appeared. Finally, in the early morning light, Ady made out the shapes of the ships themselves, unmistakably the enemy carriers.

In Simard's Midway command post, aboard Fletcher's carriers, and at Nimitz's Pearl Harbor headquarters, anxious listeners heard Ady's report:

ENEMY CARRIERS!

But that was all they heard. Ady's slow seaplane was jumped almost immediately by several Japanese fighters. Ady was too busy for the next few minutes to send any more radio messages. Finally, he managed to shake off the furious swarm of Zeros by hiding in the billowy clouds. Meanwhile a pilot in the next search sector had seen Tomonaga's attack formation departing the area. Now both went on the air:

MANY PLANES HEADING MIDWAY, BEARING 320, DISTANCE 150.

And:

TWO CARRIERS AND BATTLESHIPS, BEARING 320, DISTANCE 180, COURSE 135, SPEED 25.

In the Navy, directions are given in numbered "bearings" rather than less exact terms such as "northwest" or "south-southeast." The compass is divided into 360 degrees. A bearing of 000° is due north, 090° is east, 180° is south, and 270° is west. "Bearing 320" meant that the planes were northwest of Midway. The ships' course, reported by the second pilot as 135°, was to the southeast, toward Midway. The distances were in nautical miles, and the speed in knots.

These reports proved the wisdom of Nimitz's strategy. Yamamoto and Nagumo expected the American carriers to be in port at Pearl Harbor. The Japanese commanders were attacking from the northwest, because they thought that Midway's patrol planes would be searching to the west and southwest. But Nimitz had predicted that the attack would come from northwest—just as it had at Pearl Harbor. His three carriers, unknown to the Japanese, were lurking northeast of Midway, ready to attack the unsuspecting Nagumo's flank as his Carrier Striking Force steamed toward Midway.

Rear Admiral Frank Jack Fletcher immediately swung into action. Since *Yorktown*'s ten scouts were still in the air, he did not want to change the ship's course. If he did, the pilots would have a hard time finding their way back unless he broke radio silence to give them his new course and speed. This, of course, would warn Nagumo.

Instead, Fletcher sent a message on the VHF short-range radio to Admiral Spruance, whose Task Force 16 was about 10 miles southwest of the *Yorktown* group:

PROCEED SOUTHWESTERLY AND ATTACK ENEMY CAR-
RIERS WHEN DEFINITELY LOCATED.

The time was 6:07. Within minutes *Enterprise* and *Hornet*, with their cruiser and destroyer screen, were headed for battle.

At Midway, Captain Simard also reacted to the messages from the search planes.

Earlier that morning, Simard had sent Lieutenant Colonel Walter Sweeney of the Army Air Corps out to attack the Midway Invasion Force again with 15 Flying Fortresses. Now he radioed new orders to Sweeney:

CHANGE COURSE. ATTACK THE CARRIERS.

He ordered the rest of the planes still at Midway to

get into the air, either to take part in the battle, or—
in the case of the few PBY Catalinas still on hand—
to stay out of the way and hopefully to escape destruc-
tion in the coming attack. Marine Scout Bomber
Squadron 241 was ordered into the air, under the
command of Major Lofton R. Henderson, USMC.

Six brand-new TBF Avenger torpedo planes with
Navy pilots and four Army Air Corps B-26 Marauders, also armed with torpedoes, took off from Midway
and headed for the enemy's Carrier Striking Force.
They had to fly a roundabout course to avoid being
shot down by the incoming Japanese fighter planes.

Meanwhile, a squadron of about 25 Marine Corps
fighters, mostly obsolete Brewster Buffalos, was
scrambled to intercept the Japanese carrier planes.

Major Floyd B. Parks, commanding officer of Marine Fighter Squadron 221, led the fighters into combat. The squadron split into two groups. Parks led
eight Buffalos and five newer F4F Wildcats directly
toward the Japanese formation. Captain Kirk Armistead, his second in command, took the remaining
dozen on a course slightly to the southwest, where
they were to be held in reserve in case there should be
more than one wave of attacking planes.

Parks met the enemy at 6:16 A.M., only 30 miles
from Midway. The Marines were at 14,000 feet, 2000
feet above Tomonaga's bombers. It was obvious from
the start that the Marines were far outnumbered by
Zeros. Undaunted, they dove boldly at the attacking
bombers. Hearing Parks's contact report on his radio,

Major Floyd B. Parks, commanding officer of Midway's Marine Fighter Squadron 221.

Captain Armistead abandoned his original course and headed for the fight.

It took ten minutes for Armistead with his dozen planes to reach the scene. In that short time his squadron mates had suffered heavy losses. Parks's Buffalos were no match for the spectacular Zero fighters, which outperformed even the new Wildcats. The dogfight moved along with the Japanese bomber formation until it was over Midway. Soon Marines on the ground were supporting Marines in the air with anti-aircraft fire.

Fifteen of the Marine fighter planes went down in smoke and flame. Only ten, three of Parks's group and seven of Armistead's, survived. Of these, seven were so badly damaged that they never flew again. Floyd

Parks, the squadron commander, was one of those killed.

While the fighters scrapped overhead, the Japanese bomber formation split into two groups. One headed for Sand Island, and the other attacked Eastern Island. A few Japanese planes were shot down, but most found targets.

There were no seaplanes at anchor in the lagoon or on Sand Island's seaplane ramp, and no land planes on the strip at Eastern Island. This was a surprise to the Japanese. Lieutenant Tomonaga, believing what his admirals also believed, had counted on catching most of Midway's planes on the ground.

Finding no "sitting ducks," the Japanese turned their attention to fuel tanks, buildings, and the air-

Midway buildings damaged by Tomonaga's attack.

strip itself. The radio station, seaplane hangar, tanks, and barracks on Sand Island were heavily damaged, in spite of the fierce barrage thrown up by Navy and Marine Corps anti-aircraft gunners. On Eastern Island the power plant, mess hall, and other buildings met the same fate. Every structure on Midway, except for some underground bombproof shelters, was hit during the 20-minute attack.

But the Japanese bombs did very little damage to Eastern Island's triangle of landing runways. Seeing the airstrip surface intact, Lieutenant Tomonaga radioed back to Admiral Nagumo:

THERE IS NEED FOR A SECOND ATTACK.

His message was received on Nagumo's flagship at 7 A.M.

Tomonaga's air group had started out with 108 planes, and it was not much smaller on the return flight. The exact number of Japanese losses is not known. American accounts vary. Japanese reports also disagree, and the best Japanese estimates may not be accurate, since most of their records later were lost. One Japanese account says that only six planes failed to return from this strike. Another says that *Akagi* lost one fighter, *Hiryu* lost two attack planes in the dogfight and two more to ground fire, *Soryu* lost one attack plane, and *Kaga* lost one bomber and two fighters. This adds up to nine planes lost.

This report also says that three of *Akagi*'s fighters and nine of *Hiryu*'s fighters were damaged, two of them so badly that they could not be flown again; that four of *Kaga*'s bombers were damaged; and that all of *Soryu*'s returning planes bore bullet holes.

Whatever the exact numbers may have been, the results of the Japanese strike were heavily in Tomonaga's favor. Japanese losses in the attack were low compared to Midway's losses.

But the battle had barely begun.

Avenger

10.

Midway Strikes Back

Five minutes after Nagumo received Tomonaga's call for a second strike, the six Navy TBF Avengers and the four Army B-26 Marauders arrived over the Carrier Striking Force. Each of these Midway planes was armed with a single aerial torpedo.

Nagumo's destroyers opened up with anti-aircraft guns as soon as the ten planes approached the edge of the carrier formation. The pilots flew on, close to the water. Then the cruisers opened up, and Zeros of the carriers' combat air patrol began diving down to fire at the slower bombers.

The Zeros got three of the American planes before they were close enough to drop their torpedoes. The fourth pilot got within torpedo range, but so many fighters swarmed on his tail that he could not get into position to aim his "fish." Three more American planes were hit by anti-aircraft fire and crashed into the sea. The remaining three dropped their torpedoes but failed to score a hit. One plane nearly struck the bridge of Nagumo's flagship, the carrier *Akagi*. It passed over the Japanese carrier and then it, too, plunged into the sea. Only one Navy TBF Avenger and two Army Marauders returned to Midway.

Tomonaga's radio message and the attack by land-based planes convinced Nagumo that a second strike against Midway's airstrip really was necessary. But a third of the planes spotted on the Japanese flight decks were armed with torpedoes, deadly against ships but useless against a concrete runway. So at 7:15 A.M. Nagumo ordered *Akagi* and *Kaga*, the two carriers with torpedo planes on their flight decks, to rearm these planes with bombs.

This would be no simple task. First, plane handlers on each ship would have to push 18 planes forward, one by one, to the elevators. As quickly as they could be taken below, hangar-deck crews would have to be-

The only TBF that returned to Midway after attacking Nagumo's Carrier Striking Force the morning of June 4. Note bullet holes in wing and tail.

gin removing torpedoes and replacing them with pairs of bombs. As each plane was rearmed with bombs, it would have to be pushed to the elevator and brought topside again, where it would be spotted in its take-off position at the after end of the flight deck. The job normally would take at least two hours, but it would have to be done in half that time if the second strike was to be off the deck before 8:30. And the second strike had to be launched by that time, for at 8:30 Tomonaga's flight was due to return from its attack on Midway. Tomonaga's planes would be low on gas. Some would be damaged. More than likely, some of the pilots would be wounded. They could not be kept circling overhead, waiting for clear decks.

Nagumo had made a fateful decision. Rear Admiral Spruance already had ordered *Enterprise* and *Hornet* to begin launching their attack planes, only 200 miles over the horizon. Nagumo didn't know it, but he needed those torpedoes that his sailors were stowing below decks.

Nagumo might have known where the American carriers were if he had searched the area to the northeast more thoroughly. If Fletcher, with only three carriers, could afford to use ten planes for an early-morning search, certainly Nagumo, with four carriers, could have done as much. Instead, he chose to leave most of the scouting job to the small seaplanes carried by his cruisers. Five of these float planes and two carrier-based dive bombers were assigned search

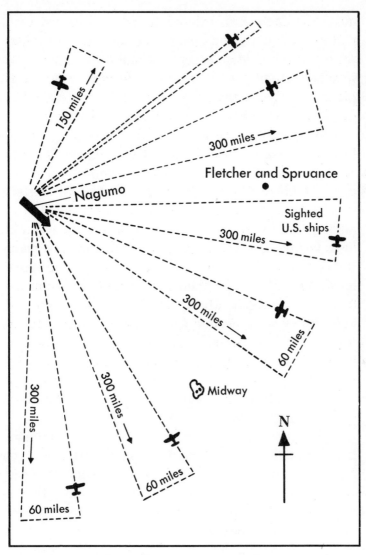

Nagumo's Early-Morning Search, June 4

missions. Each was ordered to fly a wedge-shaped pattern over the cloud-covered ocean. All the wedges were 300 miles deep, except for one to be flown by a seaplane from the battleship *Haruna*. Since this plane was smaller than the others and could carry less gas, it was to fly only 150 miles from the task force.

This was not much of a search. To weaken it even further, two of the seaplanes took off late, one because of engine trouble and the other because of a balky catapult on one of the cruisers. These late starters should have been replaced immediately by carrier planes from the second wave. In fact, Nagumo should have borrowed several planes from this reserve wave to augment the scouts. These planes could have taken off early, flown their search patterns, returned before Tomonaga's attack planes, and been refueled before they were needed again. Even if some had returned too late to take part in the second raid, a thorough search was important enough to justify weakening the second strike just a bit. For the second strike would be of little value if Nagumo did not know where his enemy was.

In Nagumo's defense, of course, it must be remembered that Admiral Yamamoto had told him that Nimitz's carriers would still be at anchor in Pearl Harbor. But this prediction was nothing more than a guess. It could be wrong. As a matter of fact, it was.

At 7:28, just a few minutes after the rearming operation had begun, Nagumo heard from one of his scouts. The news was a shock to Nagumo, and to the officers with him on his flag bridge:

TEN SHIPS, APPARENTLY ENEMY, BEARING 010, 240
MILES FROM MIDWAY. COURSE 150. SPEED MORE THAN
20 KNOTS.

The report came from one of the seaplanes which
had been launched late. If this plane had been
launched half an hour earlier, or replaced promptly
when its take-off was delayed, the contact report
might have arrived before Nagumo decided to do
without torpedoes. Now the Japanese admiral was in
an uncomfortable position. A ten-ship task force
might well include one or two carriers. If this were
the case, he'd need those "fish."

The admiral looked at his chart. The enemy force
was only about 200 miles away, well within the range
of carrier planes.

For fifteen minutes, Nagumo waited for more information. But either the seaplane pilot was being
pursued by American fighter planes or else he just
wasn't experienced enough to go closer and get a better look. Finally Nagumo issued a new order to *Akagi*
and *Kaga*:

PREPARE TO CARRY OUT ATTACKS ON ENEMY FLEET
UNITS. LEAVE TORPEDOES ON THOSE ATTACK PLANES
WHICH HAVE NOT YET BEEN CHANGED TO BOMBS.

A few minutes later, he took another chance and
broke radio silence with a short message to the seaplane scout:

ASCERTAIN SHIP TYPES AND MAINTAIN CONTACT.

But before he got his answer, his Carrier Striking
Force was visited by more United States Marines.

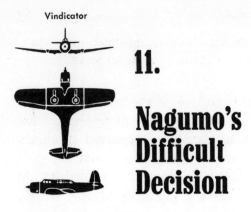

Vindicator

11.

Nagumo's Difficult Decision

Major Henderson's Scout Bomber Squadron 241 had taken off from Midway just before Tomonaga's fliers attacked the base. While Parks and Armistead flew out to intercept Tomonaga, Henderson led his 27 bombers to a point 20 miles east of Midway. They circled there, waiting for further orders. At 6:05, Lieutenant Colonel Ira Kimes, commander of Midway's Marine Aircraft Group 22, sent Henderson an urgent message:

> ATTACK ENEMY CARRIERS, BEARING 320, DISTANCE 180 MILES, COURSE 135, SPEED 20 KNOTS.

Henderson heard the order and headed for the enemy, setting his course to avoid Tomonaga's incoming raid.

Henderson's pilots were flying two different types of planes. The squadron commander himself led one section of 16 new SBD Dauntless dive bombers. Eleven older SB2U Vindicators followed with Major Benjamin W. Norris in command. Since his planes were slower than Henderson's, Norris lagged behind.

At 7:55, Henderson broke through the clouds at 9000 feet to find himself above Nagumo's task force. The carrier *Hiryu* lay directly below him.

The SBD was designed to dive at its target from an altitude of about 15,000 feet. Henderson's squadron had just received the new planes and his pilots had never practiced this difficult maneuver. Thus the major ordered an easier, more shallow glide-bombing attack, the kind his pilots had been practicing in their old Vindicators. He began to spiral down to 4000 feet.

Enemy fighters jumped the Marines even before they began their bombing runs. Along with the Zeros came a few Kates. Nagumo's carrier captains had pressed the torpedo planes into service as CAP because so many fighters had gone to Midway with Tomonaga. Looking down, the Marines could see more fighters taking off from the four carriers below them.

The Japanese pilots concentrated their attack on Henderson's plane, probably hoping that by killing the flight leader they could break up the attack. Henderson's plane began to smoke. Then it fell off its course and plunged into the sea. Captain Elmer "Ironman" Glidden took over the lead.

Anti-aircraft guns on carriers, cruisers, and destroyers opened up as the planes approached, building a wall of flak between *Hiryu* and the Marines. Zeros dove on the SBDs' tails. Still the pilots flew on. One by one they peeled off, pushing into their shallow dives about five seconds apart. Down they came, strung out in a thin, single line—fifteen planes, harassed by fighters, threatened by ack-ack, but determined to sink a carrier.

Major Henderson had been killed. Seven more of the well-named Dauntless bombers were shot down. Two of these made it partway back to Midway, however, and their crews later were picked up by patrol craft. Of eight planes that survived the attack, six were so badly damaged that they never flew again. One, flown by First Lieutenant Daniel Iverson, returned to Midway with 259 holes from flak and machine-gun bullets. Iverson's throat microphone had been shot off, and he landed the plane with no flaps and only one wheel. He later wrote in

Left: Major Lofton R. Henderson, commander of Midway's Marine Scout Bombing Squadron 241. Right: Daniel Iverson, after his promotion to captain in the Marine Corps.

his official report, "My plane was hit several times."

In spite of their bravery, Henderson's pilots didn't sink *Hiryu*. Rear-seat gunners probably shot down a few Zeros, and one pilot managed to strafe the carrier and kill a few Japanese sailors. Several of the Marines were shot down before they released their bombs. All who did release, missed, although some bombs splashed so close to the carrier that the pilots reported several hits.

At 8:10, Colonel Sweeney's 15 B-17 Flying Fortresses, which had abandoned their attack on the transports when the carriers were spotted, arrived over the Striking Force. Two of the big planes carried eight 600-pound bombs each. The other 13 were armed with eight 500-pounders apiece. Flying at 20,000 feet and bristling with machine guns, the Flying Fortresses at least were safe from Zeros and anti-aircraft guns.

The Army airmen dropped all their bombs, but with no more effect than they had had on the transports the day before. In the time it took for the bombs to fall from such a high altitude, Nagumo's skippers could zigzag out from under.

Before the B-17s had gone, Nagumo heard again from his scout:

> ENEMY SHIPS ARE FIVE CRUISERS AND FIVE DESTROY-
> ERS.

This was good news, but at 8:20 the search plane was on the air once more, this time with a much more disturbing message:

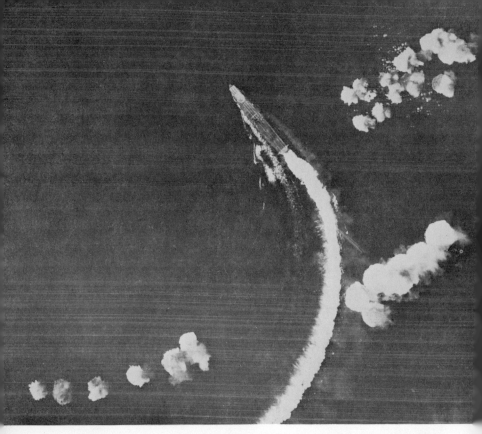

Akagi maneuvering to evade bombs from the B-17s. This photograph was taken from one of Sweeney's planes.

ENEMY FORCE ACCOMPANIED BY WHAT APPEARS TO BE AN AIRCRAFT CARRIER.

Apparently the Japanese pilot was circling over Fletcher's Task Force 17.

Along with this report came yet another air attack on Nagumo's Carrier Striking Force. Major Norris had arrived with his 11 SB2U Vindicator dive bombers. But the Japanese were ready. Fighters fell on the Marine bombers without delay. Rear-seat men shot down a pair of Zeros and may have splashed two more into the sea, but the Japanese fighters were too fast and too numerous for the Marines. Norris was driven off from the carriers and led his slow bombers into a nearby cloud.

When the Marine fliers emerged from their protective cloud, they found that they had shaken off the Zeros, at least temporarily. But now the enemy carriers were some distance away. Norris wanted a carrier, but he knew he couldn't get one. His slow, old "Vibrators," as the Marines called their planes, could never press the attack against so many fighters. Meanwhile, a Japanese battleship was directly below him.

Rather than retreat, Norris led his pilots in a shallow dive against the battleship. The tactic was no more successful this time than it had been when Henderson used it against *Hiryu*. The battleship escaped, and three Vindicators were lost. Two pilots and a gunner were rescued later.

Now a new danger threatened Nagumo. The American submarine *Nautilus*, patrolling in the area, began to pick up noise on her sonar. Lieutenant Commander William Brockman, skipper of the sub, decided to come up to periscope depth and have a look. Much to his surprise, he found himself right in the middle of Nagumo's formation. He got off a quick salvo of torpedoes. Then he dove, knowing that Japanese destroyers would head for his periscope wake at top speed, dropping depth charges—known as "ashcans" because of their size and shape—as they came.

Akagi's skipper neatly dodged Brockman's torpedoes. For the next few minutes, Japanese destroyers crossed and recrossed the spot where *Nautilus* had submerged, dropping ashcan after ashcan in an attempt to sink the submarine. *Nautilus* was rocked by several explosions uncomfortably close, but she escaped without damage. The next time Brockman came to periscope depth, he found only a single Japanese destroyer on the horizon. Nagumo had left it behind to look for the submarine when the Carrier Striking Force sailed on its way. Brockman lowered his periscope, dove deep, and made his getaway.

At 8:30 one of Nagumo's screen destroyers reported more than a hundred planes on the horizon. For a moment Nagumo thought he might be in for a few bad minutes, but the planes turned out to be Tomonaga and his Midway strike, returning to their carriers.

Again Nagumo faced a difficult decision. He knew now that the enemy had at least one carrier within striking distance. The whole purpose of his attack on Midway had been to lure the Americans into a trap. Now it looked as if Nagumo would have to attack the enemy carrier even though he was not quite ready to spring that trap.

By this time, more than half of Nagumo's torpedo planes had been rearmed with bombs for a second attack on Midway. All the fighters he had been holding back for his second attack wave had been launched to protect the task force against the Marine dive bombers led by Henderson and Norris. At this point Nagumo had only 36 dive bombers properly armed, fueled, and spotted for launching against enemy ships, plus a few Kates that still were armed with torpedoes. Meanwhile, here was Tomonaga. Most of his planes were low on fuel. Many were damaged. Some of his pilots were wounded. They needed to land just as soon as Nagumo could clear his decks.

Nagumo had three possible courses of action. He could launch the dive bombers immediately, sending them alone, without torpedo planes and with no fighter cover, to attack the American carrier task force. This would be the quickest way to attack, but the least likely to succeed. As a second choice, he could delay this strike for about half an hour, using the time to refuel some fighters and rearm a few more Kates with torpedoes. But this would require ordering Tomonaga and his tired pilots to orbit above the task force until the decks were clear. Many of them might not be able to stay aloft that long. The third possibility would be to recover Tomonaga's group now, then refuel fighters and rearm torpedo planes and launch a proper attack as soon as all the planes were ready.

This last course of action would give Nagumo the strongest possible air group, but it would take more than an hour to recover Tomonaga's planes and ready a full-scale attack. Could he afford the delay?

Again the Japanese admiral made a fateful decision. During the past hour and a half, his force had fought off torpedo planes, dive bombers, and a submarine. It had dodged more than a half-million pounds of bombs from the U.S. Army Air Corps's finest bombers. Nagumo may be forgiven for believing that his ships could take care of themselves, and for choosing the third course.

Nagumo ordered the waiting dive bombers—18 each aboard *Hiryu* and *Soryu*—wheeled forward to make landing room for Tomonaga's planes. Then he turned into the wind to recover the Midway strike. At the same time, he ordered the fighters earmarked for his second wave—which now were aloft with the combat air patrol—to land and refuel.

The torpedo planes on *Akagi's* and *Kaga's* flight decks, so recently rearmed with bombs for another strike on Midway, went below once more. There, weary and somewhat bewildered crewmen began to remove the bombs and to arm the planes with torpedoes again. This time, the job was done so hurriedly that the bombs were not even taken back to their fireproof magazines. They just were stacked in piles on the two carriers' hangar decks, to be stowed later when time would allow.

At 8:55 Nagumo sent a blinker signal to his ships:

AFTER COMPLETING RECOVERY OPERATIONS THE FORCE WILL TEMPORARILY HEAD NORTHWARD. WE PLAN TO CONTACT AND DESTROY THE ENEMY TASK FORCE.

He intended to launch 36 dive bombers, 54 torpedo planes, and a dozen fighters at 10:30 A.M. This should be more than enough fire power to sink a single enemy carrier.

Shortly before 9 o'clock Nagumo sent a short radio message to Admiral Yamamoto, who still was more than 300 miles to the west with the Main Body:

> ENEMY FORCE OF ONE CARRIER, FIVE CRUISERS, AND FIVE DESTROYERS DISCOVERED AT 8 A.M., BEARING 010, DISTANCE 240 MILES FROM MIDWAY. WE WILL HEAD FOR IT.

By 9:18, all of Tomonaga's planes were back aboard, and the Carrier Striking Force had changed course. Now it was steaming northeast at 30 knots, closing with the American force and putting additional miles between itself and Midway.

But at 9:20, Vice Admiral Nagumo saw his mistake. Destroyers and cruisers on the outer fringes of his formation began reporting enemy planes on the horizon. This time the attackers were not just a few Marines in obsolete land-based aircraft. They were carrier planes from *Enterprise* and *Hornet*. *Yorktown's* air group was not far behind.

The tide was turning. The Battle of Midway had begun in earnest, and Nagumo was no longer the aggressor.

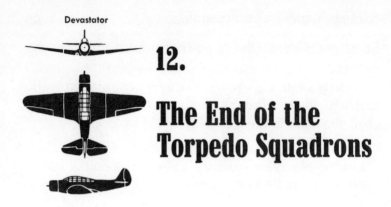

Devastator

12.

The End of the Torpedo Squadrons

Rear Admiral Raymond Spruance had set his course toward the southwest at a few minutes past 6 A.M., to get Task Force 16 within striking distance of the Japanese carriers. Plotting Nagumo's position on his navigation chart, he saw that the enemy was less than 200 miles away. At a speed of 25 knots he might reduce that distance to about 100 miles by 9 A.M. That was the hour at which he intended to order *Enterprise* and *Hornet* to launch their air groups.

As the bows of his ships cut through the blue-green sea, the admiral began to receive reports of Lieutenant Tomonaga's attack on Midway. Captain Miles Browning, Spruance's chief of staff, calculated that the Japanese fliers would be returning to their carriers sometime between 8:30 and 9. If Spruance's torpedo planes and dive bombers were to attack then, they might catch the Japanese carriers at the moment of recovery, when their extra fighter planes would be down below, in the hangar decks. Better yet, Nagumo's flight decks might be jammed with aircraft being refueled and rearmed. There would be no time when Nagumo would be in a worse position to defend his task force from attack.

To attack by 9 A.M., however, would require Spruance's carriers to launch at 7 o'clock, when they would be more than 150 miles from their targets. Allowing for the time the pilots would have to fly at top speed during the attack, such a long approach would leave them barely enough gas for the return flight. Some, in fact, might be forced to land in the sea, somewhere between the enemy and Task Force 16.

Fletcher's orders to Spruance meant only one thing: sink carriers. To carry out these orders meant risking American lives, no matter when he launched. If Spruance waited his task force, too, might be found by a scout plane. In that case, he might lose his carriers as well as his planes. If he were to launch early, he would have a good chance of surprising Nagumo and sinking much or all of the enemy's Carrier Striking Force. And if he were to sink the Japanese carriers, he could safely send destroyers and Midway's seaplanes out to rescue any of his own pilots who might be floating in rubber rafts on the sea.

He debated the question with Browning and the other members of his staff. But a staff can only help. The task-force commander must make the hard decisions himself. The responsibility is his, and his alone. No one else would have to answer for the success of the mission or the lives lost in carrying out his orders.

Spruance made the decision. His carriers would launch at 7 o'clock.

Enterprise and *Hornet* were steaming in formation, protected by their screen of cruisers and destroyers. Now they had to separate in order to give the fliers air room, and they had to turn into the wind, away from the enemy. Three cruisers, *Northampton*, *Pensacola*, and *Vincennes*, stayed with *Enterprise*, along with five destroyers. *Hornet* formed a separate task group, with the cruisers *Minneapolis*, *New Orleans*, and *Atlanta* and four destroyers.

The first planes in the air were the F4F Wildcats. These stubby little fighters were less than 30 feet long and had a wingspan of only 38 feet. The Wildcat's top speed in level flight was 285 knots, the same as the Japanese Zero's. It was armed with six forward-firing machine guns. Like the Japanese Zero, the F4F was flown by one man, who was pilot, radioman, and gunner. The Wildcat was a rugged little plane. Like its namesake, it could stay in a fight and take a lot of punishment. But it was outgunned by the Zero, which also could outclimb and outmaneuver it.

Dive bombers and torpedo planes followed the fighters off the carrier decks. The dive bombers were SBD Dauntless models, just like those flown by Major Henderson's Midway-based Marines. The Dauntless was a two-seater, carrying a radioman-gunner who rode behind the pilot. It was four feet longer and had four feet more wingspan than the Wildcat, flew 65 knots slower, and carried either a 1000-pound bomb

SBD Dauntless dive bomber (foreground) and obsolete TBD Devastators ready to launch from *Enterprise.*

or two 500-pounders. The pilot controlled a pair of .50-caliber machine guns that fired forward through the propeller. His crewman had a single .30-caliber gun which could be fired aft or to either side. In later models this was a twin mount. The SBD was used as a scout as well as for dive bombing. For search missions it usually carried extra gasoline and a smaller bomb load, or no bombs at all.

Enterprise was only a week away from the day on which her torpedo squadron was scheduled to receive its new TBF Avengers. The TBF was a tough, 240-knot plane that the Navy would continue to use throughout World War II. But during the Battle of Midway both *Enterprise*'s and *Hornet*'s torpedo squadrons still were flying the older TBD Devas-

tator, a three-place, 170-knot torpedo bomber. The
Devastator was armed with only one fixed machine
gun forward and one turret gun aft. It carried either
1200 pounds of bombs or a single aerial torpedo.

Standard Navy tactics called for the dive bombers
and fighters to arrive first at the target ships. The dive
bombers climbed to about 15,000 feet, with the fighters staying about 5000 feet above them. Then the dive
bombers pushed over into their almost vertical dives,
releasing their bombs at about 3000 feet or less and
pulling out to escape at masthead level, too low to be
hit by enemy anti-aircraft guns. By staying high the
fighters kept an advantage over enemy fighters, which
could not climb as fast as the Wildcats could dive.

As the attack developed, both the enemy's fighter
planes and his shipboard gunners could be expected
to concentrate on the dive bombers. Meanwhile, the
slower, more vulnerable torpedo planes could come
in at a very low altitude, almost brushing the crests of
the waves with their wings, to launch their torpedoes
as close as possible to the target ships.

This is not quite what happened at Midway.

The first planes to reach the spot where the enemy
had last been seen were two squadrons of SBDs, es-
corted by ten fighters. They were led by Commander
Stanhope C. Ring, commander of *Hornet*'s air group.
But Nagumo had changed course to close with the
Yorktown task force, and not a ship was in sight.

Ring did not know that *Yorktown* had been
spotted, and he had no idea that Nagumo had decided

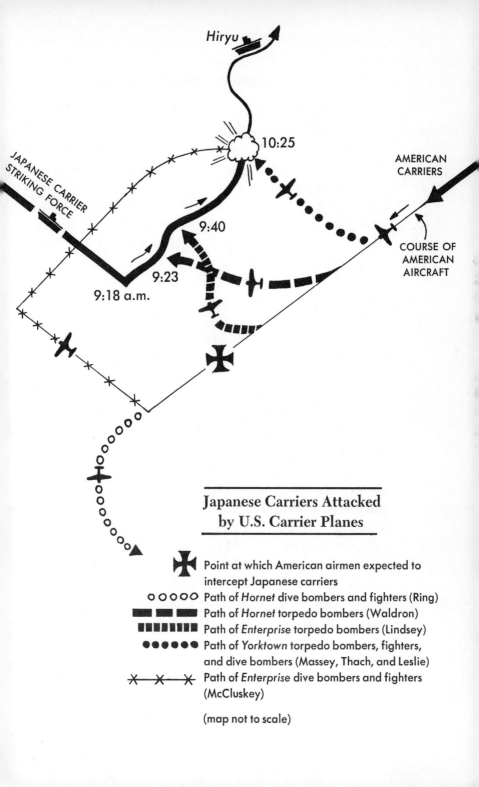

Hiryu

10:25

JAPANESE CARRIER
STRIKING FORCE

9:40

9:23

9:18 a.m.

AMERICAN
CARRIERS

COURSE OF
AMERICAN
AIRCRAFT

Japanese Carriers Attacked
by U.S. Carrier Planes

✠ Point at which American airmen expected to intercept Japanese carriers

○○○○○ Path of *Hornet* dive bombers and fighters (Ring)

■ ■ ■ Path of *Hornet* torpedo bombers (Waldron)

▬▬▬ Path of *Enterprise* torpedo bombers (Lindsey)

●●●●● Path of *Yorktown* torpedo bombers, fighters, and dive bombers (Massey, Thach, and Leslie)

✕—✕—✕ Path of *Enterprise* dive bombers and fighters (McCluskey)

(map not to scale)

to sail north. Instead, he guessed that the Japanese had headed south to launch a second strike against Midway. So Ring made a wide left turn and led his 35 dive bombers and ten Wildcats off in a futile search, thereby missing the rest of the battle. Thirteen of his SBDs ran so low on fuel that they had to land at Midway. Two crash-landed in the lagoon. All ten fighters had to ditch at sea, and only eight of the fighter pilots were rescued.

Lieutenant Commander John C. Waldron's Torpedo Squadron Eight was supposed to be part of Ring's attack group, but his low-flying TBD Devastators became separated from the higher-flying SBDs and F4Fs by clouds shortly after leaving *Hornet*. They missed Ring's turn to the south. Arriving at the target's assumed position, Waldron found himself on his own.

This was no new experience for John Waldron, Annapolis graduate, part Sioux Indian, and a naval aviator since 1927. He was a natural flier and a born leader, devoted to his country, his men, and his profession. In the months his squadron had been together, Waldron had welded the group into a tight, tough team. Many of his pilots were Naval Reserve officers, recently called to active duty. Most had little experience but all, like Waldron, were ready.

The night before the battle, Waldron had written a note to his squadron and attached it to his battle plan. "My greatest hope," he wrote, "is that we will encounter a favorable tactical situation. But if we don't and the worst comes to the worst, I want each of us to do his utmost to destroy our enemies. If there is only one plane left to make a final run-in, I want that man to go in and get a hit. May God be with us all."

Waldron guessed that Nagumo had turned north. He followed, and his were the first American carrier planes to find Nagumo's Striking Force.

As the 15 torpedo bombers approached the outer fringes of Nagumo's formation, the Japanese admiral ordered all available fighters into the air. More than 50 Zeros fell on the slow Devastators. But Waldron bored on in, against a hail of machine-gun bullets and a heavy barrage from the larger guns of cruisers and destroyers.

Now the worst had come. With no fighter cover, compelled to fly a straight course in order to aim their torpedoes, the old, slow TBDs were easy targets for the Japanese fighter pilots. Waldron's plane was one of the first hit. Flames shot up from his bullet-pierced gas tanks as the plane skimmed a few yards above the water. In a desperate attempt to escape, the squadron commander opened his canopy and stood up in the cockpit. Just then, the plane hit the water. It was traveling at more than 100 miles an hour. When the spray had settled, Waldron and his Devastator were gone.

Torpedo Squadron Eight flew on. Zeros dove from above. Bullets tore through planes and flesh, but Waldron's pilots refused to turn back. One by one, 14 planes fell flaming into the sea. Suddenly Ensign George Gay, the formation's "tail end Charlie," found himself alone with his tail gunner against four carriers and 50 enemy fighters. A bullet crashed through his armored cockpit and struck him in the arm. Gay pinched it out and kept flying. His gunner cried out, "I'm hit!" and died. Gay flew on. With his target directly ahead, he pressed the torpedo release. The damaged mechanism jammed. Gay reached for the manual release cable, jerked it, and felt the plane jump as the heavy torpedo fell free.

A small shell exploded in the cockpit, tearing away the rudder controls and burning Gay's leg. The shattered aircraft hurtled across the bow of an enemy carrier and crashed into the sea. Gay's torpedo, its aim thrown off when the electric release failed, missed the ship.

Left: Lieutenant Commander John C. Waldron, commander of *Hornet's* Torpedo Squadron Eight. Right: Ensign George Gay, sole survivor of Waldron's squadron, in the hospital at Pearl Harbor after the Battle of Midway.

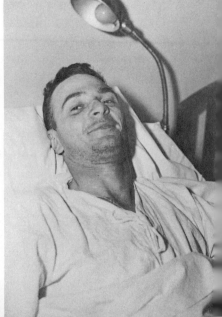

Miraculously, Gay found himself able to swim away from the sinking plane. He inflated his life vest and swam to a bag containing a deflated rubber raft, which had floated free from the plane. A seat cushion also was floating nearby. Gay pulled the cushion over his head to make sure he would not be seen and strafed by any of the enemy pilots still circling overhead.

Gay floated that way for the rest of the day, watching the battle until it disappeared over the horizon. After dark he inflated his life raft and climbed aboard. A PBY passed over him on a search mission the next morning, spotted him, and picked him up on its way back to Midway that afternoon.

Ensign Gay was the only survivor of Torpedo Squadron Eight. A few days later, at Pearl Harbor Naval Hospital, a doctor asked him how he had treated his wounds while waiting to be rescued. Gay replied calmly that he had soaked them in salt water for several hours.

The squadrons from the carrier *Enterprise* also became separated during the long flight. Lieutenant Commander Eugene Lindsey's Torpedo Squadron Six arrived unescorted at 9:30, just a few minutes after Waldron's attack. Lindsey saw no friendly planes, but there were plenty of targets. Wasting no time, he led his 13 fellow pilots in another brave but futile torpedo attack. As Lindsey headed for *Kaga*'s broad port side, the Zeros began to swarm. At least two fell on each TBD.

Lindsey's pilots were as brave as Waldron's. Most

met the same fate. Only four out of 14 survived. Every man who had not been shot down—and some who later were—stuck it out to the launch point and dropped his "fish." But not one pilot scored a hit.

Yorktown had long since recovered her scouts, and Admiral Fletcher had ordered Task Force 17 to head for the battle. Shortly after 8:30, on Fletcher's orders, Captain Buckmaster had launched a dozen torpedo bombers, 17 dive bombers, and six fighters. The launch was completed in about half an hour, and at 9:06 the planes headed for the enemy carriers.

Commander Oscar Pederson, commander of *Yorktown's* air group, had come up with his own analysis of the situation. He assumed that the Japanese would still be heading southwest, toward Midway. He ordered his pilots to assume that the enemy carriers were steaming at their very top speed, and to set their course to intercept on that assumption. When they reached the rendezvous point, if the carriers were not there the pilots were to assume that they had over-estimated the enemy's speed, and change their own course to the northwest. If the enemy was still heading for Midway, the pilots would find them.

As it happened, the enemy was no longer heading for Midway, but the strategy worked anyway. Instead of approaching Nagumo's carriers from dead ahead, the *Yorktown* fliers caught up with the enemy from astern.

The torpedo bombers came first. Lieutenant Commander Lance Massey, skipper of *Yorktown's* Torpedo

Squadron Three, saw smoke on the horizon ahead and about 30 degrees to his right. He changed course to starboard and headed for the fight.

Massey was luckier than Waldron or Lindsey. At least he had some fighter protection from Lieutenant Commander John S. Thach and his half-dozen Wildcats, flying 5000 feet above him. But seven torpedo planes, including Massey's, crashed into the sea without launching their torpedoes. Five managed to launch, but three of them also went down in flames. There just were too many Zeros for "Jimmy" Thach and his fighters to dispose of, and enemy anti-aircraft fire was too accurate for the slow TBDs to dodge.

In all, 41 planes from three carrier-based torpedo squadrons had attacked Nagumo's carriers. Only six

Two of *Yorktown's* squadron commanders: Lieutenant Commander Lance Massey of Torpedo Squadron Three (left), and Lieutenant Commander John S. Thach of Fighter Squadron Three.

returned. More than 30 pilots and as many gunners were killed. Yet not a single torpedo had struck an enemy ship.

But the torpedo bombers were not sacrificed in vain. They had forced Nagumo to launch the fighters he was saving for his strike against *Yorktown,* and to delay the launch of his own dive bombers and torpedo bombers. The Japanese carriers, maneuvering desperately to escape from the relentless attack, had broken their formation. Now they were scattered widely. And the low-flying TBDs had drawn all of Nagumo's Zeros down to such a low altitude that they were out of position to defend the carriers against the next attack.

The next attack was only minutes away.

13.

The Dive Bombers Score

All during the torpedo attacks, crewmen on Nagumo's four carriers were working frantically to refuel fighters and rearm torpedo planes for the next round of the battle. At 10:20, Nagumo ordered his carrier captains to begin launching as soon as possible. His own flagship began to turn into the wind. At 10:24, *Akagi's* air officer raised his white flag and the first plane roared off her bow.

At that moment, high above the Japanese carriers, 17 SBD Dauntless dive bombers from USS *Yorktown* were just beginning their dives.

Lieutenant Commander Maxwell Leslie's Bombing Squadron Three had taken off from *Yorktown* at about 9 A.M. Following Commander Pederson's orders, Leslie flew to a spot southeast of Nagumo's probable position and then set his course to the northwest. Leslie arrived over the Japanese carriers just minutes after the end of Massey's torpedo attack.

Through a quirk of fate not all of Leslie's planes still had their bombs. The SBDs recently had been equipped with a new electric bomb release. Shortly after take-off, the pilots "armed" their bombs. This meant disconnecting the safety mechanism so that the bomb would drop when the pilot pressed the release button. To the pilots' dismay, three of the planes dropped their bombs into the sea the moment the safeties were cut out. The first pilot to lose his weapons was Max Leslie.

This was a bitter blow. Leslie was an experienced naval officer who had spent 20 years in the service of his country. Now, with an opportunity to sink an enemy carrier and perhaps help change the course of the war, he found himself entering the battle armed only with machine guns. His .50-caliber guns could hardly do much damage to a 20,000-ton ship, but there was no turning back. So Leslie led the squadron resolutely on, till ships appeared on the horizon ahead. Then he shopped for a target, picked a big one, and led the attack. This time, the pilots of the American squadron were not attacking alone.

Lieutenant Commander Clarence Wade McClusky, commander of the *Enterprise* air group, had taken off at a few minutes after 7:00 that morning leading more than 30 SBDs. Fifteen were armed with single 1000-pound bombs. The rest each carried one 500-pound bomb and a pair of 200-pounders. Like Ring and Waldron, McClusky arrived at Nagumo's reported position and found nothing below him but a peaceful ocean. Where Ring had turned south and missed the battle, and Waldron had turned north and found it, Wade McClusky kept his dive bombers on a steady course for a few more minutes. Then he guessed that perhaps the enemy had found Fletcher's carriers and was steaming north to attack them. Acting on this hunch McClusky, too, turned north. A few minutes later he saw the wake of a single ship steaming north at high speed.

This was the Japanese destroyer *Arashi,* the ship Nagumo had left behind earlier that morning to search for the American submarine *Nautilus.* The Japanese destroyer skipper, not having any luck as a subchaser, was heading back to rejoin the carriers. McClusky had no idea why the destroyer was steaming alone, but he guessed where she was heading. He changed his own course slightly and flew on in exactly the same direction that the destroyer was heading. He sighted the enemy carriers just as Max Leslie's *Yorktown* SBDs were diving at one of the Japanese flat-tops from an altitude of 14,500 feet.

There still is some question whether Leslie attacked the 688-foot *Soryu* or the 715-foot *Kaga.* Before the slaughter of the torpedo planes, Nagumo's four carriers had been steaming in a diamond-shaped formation, with cruisers and destroyers outboard to protect them against aircraft or submarines. During the torpedo attacks the orderly formation had broken up. Now *Soryu, Akagi,* and *Kaga* were steaming fairly close to each other in a triangle-shaped formation. *Hiryu* and her escorts were in a separate group several miles to the north. Most reports written at the time say that Leslie's Bombing Squadron Three attacked *Soryu.*

Later accounts, written after more detailed study of all the evidence, generally agree that Leslie's victim was *Kaga*. Leslie's own battle report says that his planes attacked a large carrier with its superstructure on the starboard side of the flight deck. Since *Akagi* and *Kaga* both were larger than *Soryu*, and *Akagi*'s island was on the port side, it seems most likely that Leslie's large carrier with its island to starboard was *Kaga*.

Whoever attacked her, *Kaga* soon was a mass of flames. Four bombs, probably all 1000-pounders, ripped through her flight deck and exploded below. The blast from one of these bomb explosions shot down a plane that was just taking off from the carrier's flight deck. A gasoline truck parked on the flight deck burst into flames. A geyser of burning gasoline erupted over the island, instantly killing Captain Jisaku Okada and everyone else on the bridge. Flames spread in burning rivers to planes parked on the flight deck. Burning gasoline poured through bomb holes in the flight deck down into the ship's interior. Bombs and torpedoes on the burning planes exploded with terrible results. The intense heat also set off bombs which had been left stacked on the hangar deck the last time the torpedo planes were rearmed.

Commander Takahisa Amagai, *Kaga*'s air officer, took command of the stricken ship. *Kaga*'s crew tried bravely to save her, but in less than four hours the Emperor's portrait had to be transferred to a destroyer. At 4:40 that afternoon Commander Amagai finally gave the order to abandon ship. Earlier in the afternoon

SBD Dauntless dive bombers in action at the Battle of Midway, above a burning Japanese ship. This is enlarged from a Navy 16-mm motion-picture film.

a submarine, probably *Nautilus*, had fired three torpedoes at the burning carrier. Two missed. The third hit, broke in two, and failed to explode. Several members of *Kaga*'s crew who had already gone over the side managed to stay afloat by hanging on to the torpedo's afterbody. Now the rest of *Kaga*'s crew left the ship, most to be picked up immediately by destroyers. Later, when the fires seemed to be dying down, Commander Amagai led a salvage party back aboard, but he was forced to abandon the effort in less than an hour.

At 7:25 P.M. *Kaga*'s hull was ripped by two tremendous explosions, one forward and the other aft. The fire had reached her fuel tanks. Minutes later, the shattered hull slipped beneath the waves, leaving a billowing tower of black smoke behind to mark the once powerful carrier's grave. The bodies of 800 crewmen, killed in battle or trapped by fire, went to the bottom with the ship. So did nearly all her planes.

The two carriers steaming in formation with *Kaga* were attacked at just about the same time she was. McClusky divided his planes into two sections. One dove at *Akagi*, Nagumo's flagship. If it really was *Kaga* that Leslie attacked, then McClusky's second section must have dropped its bombs on *Soryu*.

Three bombs tore through *Soryu*'s flight deck. One hit forward, one amidships, and one aft. They could not have been better aimed. In seconds, the carrier was a mass of flames. In 20 minutes, her captain gave the order to abandon ship. He stayed aboard, however, preferring death on his own bridge to rescue. All efforts to get him to leave were met with failure. He was last seen standing on his shattered bridge, his sword in his hand, singing the Japanese national anthem as smoke billowed about him and flames engulfed the carrier's island. The ruined ship stayed afloat for about seven hours, with fires raging from bow to stern. Explosions erupted from time to time, as the searing heat ignited fuel tanks and ammunition magazines. Shortly after seven that evening, *Soryu* plunged to the bottom of the Pacific.

Only two bombs struck *Akagi,* Admiral Nagumo's flagship. But armed planes on her flight and hangar decks caught fire, and bombs, stacked where hangar deck crews had left them during the rearming operation, began to explode. Flames reached the gasoline tanks of parked aircraft. The tanks exploded, spraying burning gasoline in all directions and turning the hangar deck into an inferno. Torpedoes on loaded planes blew up, shattering bulkheads with fearful concussions and scattering flames throughout the ship.

Admiral Nagumo's staff pleaded with him to leave the carrier. He still had the Striking Force to command, and the undamaged cruiser *Nagara* was standing by to take him aboard. Finally the admiral reluctantly agreed. By that time all the passageways down from the bridge were filled with flames. The admiral and his staff had to go out one of the bridge windows and climb down a rope to the flight deck. Then they made their way forward and climbed down a rope ladder to a waiting launch.

Captain Taijiro Aoki, commanding officer of *Akagi,* carried on the fight to save the ship. The engine room had not been hit and the big carrier still had power and lights. Soon pumps began to fail, however, and then the flames reached the electrical generators. Lights flickered, dimmed, and went out. All communications went dead. Officers and enlisted men of the ship's engineering department, who had bravely stayed at their stations knowing that the ship had been badly damaged, now were trapped below. Fire cut off their escape routes, and every attempt to rescue them failed.

During the afternoon the Emperor's portrait was removed from its position of honor. A ceremonial guard carried it to the side of the ship, where it was transferred to a waiting destroyer. In the early evening all hands were ordered to abandon ship. Captain Aoki asked Vice Admiral Nagumo for permission to sink the flaming ship with torpedoes in order to prevent her from falling into American hands. Admiral Yamamoto heard Aoki's radio message and ordered him to wait; perhaps the ship might be saved. But at 3:50 the next morning Yamamoto reluctantly agreed. Nagumo issued the orders, and four Japanese destroyers fired torpedoes at the stricken flagship. The last torpedo was fired at 4:46 A.M. Seven minutes later she disappeared beneath the waves.

The dive-bomber attack had taken only five minutes. Since early morning, Nagumo's Carrier Striking Force had withstood bombs and torpedoes from carrier planes, land-based aircraft, and a submarine. Some of the missiles had been dodged. A good many of the attack planes had been shot down. An enemy carrier had been found, and Nagumo was about to attack it. Now, in less time than it would take to walk from the bow of his proud flagship to her stern, what was to be Japan's greatest naval victory had slipped from Vice Admiral Nagumo's grasp.

Val

14.

Yorktown's Ordeal

At the moment the American dive bombers attacked, Nagumo had been preparing to launch a strike against *Yorktown.* Now three of Nagumo's four carriers had been hit, but the Japanese Striking Force was not yet out of the fight. Rear Admiral Abe in the cruiser *Tone* temporarily took command of the Striking Force while Vice Admiral Nagumo transferred to the cruiser *Nagara.* At 10:50 A.M. Abe sent a radio message to Admiral Yamamoto, telling the Commander in Chief that *Akagi, Kaga,* and *Soryu* were out of action, but that he was going to attack the American task force immediately with *Hiryu's* planes. Then Abe ordered Rear Admiral Yamaguchi, Commander Carrier Division Two, to launch the attack.

Yamaguchi was one of the most promising officers in the Japanese Navy. Although he was younger than many other rear admirals, he was considered a likely successor to Admiral Yamamoto as Commander in Chief of the Combined Fleet. He had been a trusted friend of Yamamoto's for a number of years, and was one of the first officers with whom Yamamoto discussed his plans for an attack on Pearl Harbor. Like Yamamoto, he had served as the Japanese naval attaché in Washington. He was a wise, bold leader who knew his enemy and was respected and loved by his men.

As might be expected, Yamaguchi had not waited for Abe's orders. *Hiryu* already was launching aircraft when Abe's message arrived.

Eighteen Vals and six Zeros took off from *Hiryu's* flight deck. They were led by Lieutenant Michio Kobayashi, commanding officer of one of *Hiryu's* dive-bombing squadrons. Kobayashi was an experienced pilot, who had flown in the attack on Pearl Harbor with Nagumo's Striking Force and in the Indian Ocean. As the planes climbed to their cruising altitude, they were joined by two scouts from the cruiser *Chikuma*. The scout pilots had found *Yorktown* earlier. Now they were to lead the dive bombers to the target. Kobayashi also got an assist from American dive bombers returning to *Yorktown*, which unwittingly showed him the direction of Fletcher's task force.

Meanwhile, to the south, Vice Admiral Kondo turned over command of the Invasion Force to Vice Admiral Kurita. Then, taking a pair of battleships, the light carrier *Zuiho*, and several cruisers and destroyers, he broke away from the transports and headed northeast at 28 knots. At that speed, he could expect to reach the battle area in nine or ten hours. At the same time Admiral Yamamoto ordered the light car-

riers *Ryujo* and *Junyo*, which had been supporting the
invasion of the Aleutians, as well as the Aleutian
Screening Force of battleships and cruisers, to steam
south and join what was left of Nagumo's Carrier
Striking Force.

The Japanese Combined Fleet had been badly hurt,
but Yamamoto was not ready to admit defeat.

And, at one minute before noon, Kobayashi found
Yorktown.

Rear Admiral Fletcher had ordered Captain Buckmaster to launch ten scout planes about an hour earlier.
Now flight-deck crews were refueling ten fighters—
six of the ship's combat air patrol and four that had
just returned from the battle. Thirteen SBD Dauntless
dive bombers were spotted on *Yorktown's* flight deck,
waiting to be called away for the next strike. Seven
more SBDs with 1000-pound bombs and full gas tanks
were parked in her hangar deck. This was the situation when radar picked up the approaching Japanese.

The 12 fighters already in the air were ordered out
to intercept the attackers. On deck, fueling was
stopped immediately. An 800-gallon auxiliary tank
full of aviation gasoline, which had been parked near
the after end of the flight deck, was pushed over the
side. Gasoline was drained from pipelines running
from storage tanks below the water line up to the flight
deck and hangar deck. The entire fueling system was
pumped full of carbon-dioxide gas as a precaution
against fires.

Max Leslie's returning dive bombers had just

formed a circle at about 500 feet, from which they would peel off one by one to land on the carrier. Buckmaster ordered Leslie to stay in the air. Those of Leslie's planes that still had ammunition for their forward guns joined the CAP.

The engine room built the ship's speed up from 25 knots to 30½—not bad for a ship that had been damaged so badly less than a month before in the Battle of the Coral Sea. Rear Admiral William W. Smith, screen commander of Task Force 17, stationed his cruisers and destroyers in a ring two miles in diameter with the carrier at the center, to give gunfire support.

One of Admiral Fletcher's aides stepped up to tell him the enemy planes were drawing near. "Well, I've got my tin hat on," the admiral replied. "I can't do anything else now!"

Now it was up to fighter pilots and anti-aircraft gunners.

Jimmy Thach's fighters, now flying CAP, fell on the enemy dive bombers while they were still 20 miles from *Yorktown*. They shot down at least half of the Vals. Several more Vals and Zeros were knocked out of the sky by gunners on *Yorktown* and the ships of her screen. But at least a half-dozen Vals dived at the carrier as Captain Buckmaster put the ship through a series of zigzagging turns in an effort to dodge their bombs.

The first bomb missed the ship. It exploded in the water close aboard the starboard side, near enough to jar the carrier and spray her decks with salt water but

Yorktown's flight deck minutes after the dive-bomber attack. Smoke pouring from stack was caused by bomb hits which damaged boilers.

too far away to cause any damage. The plane that dropped it was shot down as the pilot pulled out of his dive.

The next two bombs hit. One fell from a Val which already had been hit by anti-aircraft fire. The plane was blown apart and one of its wings landed on *Yorktown's* flight deck, but the bomb fell true. It tore through the flight deck and exploded in the hangar deck. Three planes parked there immediately burst into flames. The ship would have been an inferno within seconds except for prompt action by Lieutenant A. C. Emerson, whose damage-control station was nearby. He quickly turned on a sprinkler system which put out the fire. He was too late, however, to save several men who were killed by the explosion. The bomb also knocked a number of anti-aircraft guns out of action, and the hole in *Yorktown*'s flight deck would prevent any more landings or take-offs until it could be patched.

The other Japanese bomb ripped through the flight deck diagonally and pierced the wall of the smokestack below decks. It exploded inside the smokestack, tearing open the engine-room uptakes—huge tubes that carry smoke from the boilers to the stacks. Boiler rooms and nearby compartments were filled with hot, choking gases which drove boilermen away from their stations. Two of the ship's six working boilers were badly damaged, and the fires in three others were blown out. The ship began to lose speed.

One pilot leveled off and flew close aboard the ship, thumbing his nose as he pulled out of his steep dive. His triumph was brief, however. Seconds later *Yorktown*'s anti-aircraft gunners got him in their sights. A direct hit blew off the tail of his plane, and the Val plunged into the sea.

The fourth bomb dropped—the third to hit— started fires below decks on the starboard side. The ship seemed doomed, and the eight enemy pilots who returned to *Hiryu* triumphantly told Admiral Yamaguchi that they had sunk an American carrier.

The attack cost the Japanese 13 dive bombers and three Zeros. Lieutenant Kobayashi was among those who failed to return.

Yorktown was not sunk, but the damage was serious.

By 12:20 all engines were stopped and the big ship lay dead in the water. Flames from fires near the island had damaged communications and radar equipment. Fletcher was not ready to count *Yorktown* out, but the crippled ship obviously could no longer serve as his flagship. He signaled Admiral Smith in the cruiser *Astoria* to send a boat for him and his staff. The sea was calm, and *Astoria*'s motor whaleboat soon was alongside. One by one, the officers of Fletcher's staff lowered themselves 75 feet down a rope from the carrier's flight deck to the waiting boat. Fletcher, who was nearly 57 years old, started to follow. With one leg over the side, he muttered, "I'm too old for this sort of thing!" and climbed back aboard. Sailors quickly bent a bowline knot on the end of a line and lowered the Admiral without ceremony into the waiting boat.

Captain Buckmaster's well-trained crew did a magnificent job fighting fires. Meanwhile *Yorktown* planes still in the air were ordered to land on *Enterprise* or *Hornet*. Most of the battle-scarred SBDs made it, but Max Leslie and his wingman, "Lefty" Holmberg, ran out of gas. They ditched close to *Astoria*. Leslie and his crewman climbed out of their battered plane into a rubber raft, and soon were picked up by one of *Astoria*'s motorboats. Holmberg also was saved, but only after a swim. He and his crewman stepped into their life raft just as their plane sank. But the raft was full of bullet holes, and better suited for holding water than for holding air. It went down almost as fast as the

Maxwell Leslie, commander of *Yorktown's* Bombing Squadron Three, had to ditch near *Astoria*. Below: The cruiser sent its motor whaleboat to pick up Leslie and his crewman.

plane. Fortunately both men were wearing inflatable life vests, which kept them afloat until a boat reached them.

By 2:00 *Yorktown* damage-control crews had repaired her torn uptakes and patched up the jagged holes in her flight deck. Four boilers were back "on the line," and her engines were turning up 20 knots. Admiral Spruance had sent two cruisers and a pair of destroyers to strengthen *Yorktown*'s anti-aircraft and anti-submarine screen, and a number of fighters to fly CAP. Now the carrier was fueling her own fighters on deck. *Yorktown* was back in the fight.

Since 8:20 that morning, when the cruiser *Chikuma*'s scout finally identified *Yorktown*, the Japanese admirals had thought they were up against only one carrier. But in the early afternoon they learned the truth from the pilot of a scout plane launched hours earlier by *Soryu*. Finding *Soryu* in flames, the pilot landed on *Hiryu*. Then he rushed to Admiral Yamaguchi's bridge and reported that he had seen not just one but three enemy carriers. But his radio had broken down and he had been unable to report his find sooner. He identified the ships correctly as *Enterprise, Hornet,* and *Yorktown.*

Yamaguchi ordered all the planes he had ready— ten torpedo planes and six fighters—to attack *Hornet* and *Enterprise.* They took off at 12:45. One of the Kates was from *Akagi*'s air group and two of the Zeros came from *Kaga.* They had landed on *Hiryu* earlier when their own carriers were under attack.

Damage-control men repairing hole in *Yorktown* flight deck after the dive-bomber attack.

This last Japanese attack was led by Lieutenant Tomonaga, commander of the early-morning strike against Midway. Tomonaga's plane had been damaged that morning and the left wing tank still had not been repaired. But he refused to stay behind, although he knew he had almost no chance of returning from this attack.

The strike arrived at 2:30. By chance Tomonaga failed to find *Hornet* and *Enterprise*. Instead, he came on *Yorktown*. The carrier was steaming under her own power. From the air, she showed no evidence of the wounds she had suffered during Kobayashi's attack. Naturally, Tomonaga mistook her for an undamaged carrier.

Once again *Yorktown*'s flight-deck crews stopped

fueling planes. Six fighters already aloft were sent to intercept the attackers. Eight partly gassed fighters, led by Jimmy Thach, took off to join the dogfight, although their tanks held an average of only 20 gallons of fuel. Again the ship's aviation-gas pipes were filled with carbon dioxide. Again damage-control men stood by their stations, knowing that if the ship were hit once more their job would be nearly hopeless. Gunners on all ships in the task force pointed their weapons toward the sky.

Wildcat fighters intercepted Tomonaga about ten miles from the carrier. Zeros dove at Wildcats while Wildcats dove at Kates. Meanwhile, Tomonaga's torpedo planes scattered to attack *Yorktown* from several directions at once. Thach's fighters followed the torpedo planes. Cruisers and destroyers opened up with their anti-aircraft guns. Rear Admiral Smith's cruisers depressed their 8-inch main battery guns to fire into the sea ahead of the torpedo planes. The huge shells exploded as they hit the waves, throwing up a nearly solid wall of water in the path of the low-flying planes.

The action moved so quickly that one of *Yorktown*'s fighters took off, engaged a Val, was shot up by a Zero, and crashed, all in the space of a minute. The pilot had not even had time to raise his landing gear, which in those days had to be cranked up by hand. Fortunately he managed to climb high enough to bail out safely. He was picked up by a destroyer a few minutes later. This was the young officer's first flight in combat and

Water spurts into the air as a Japanese torpedo hits *Yorktown*.

one of the shortest on record. A newspaper reporter later asked him if he had been frightened. "Not until I got aboard that destroyer," he answered. "Then I was afraid it might sink!"

Several of the attacking planes were shot down, some of them before they could launch their torpedoes. Tomonaga managed to drop his, just as he flew into what one of the Japanese pilots later called "the heaviest anti-aircraft fire I have ever seen." Tomonaga's plane was hit and exploded, seconds after the brave airman launched his "fish."

Four torpedoes headed straight for *Yorktown*. Captain Buckmaster managed to dodge two of them, but the other two struck the port side of the carrier, blasting huge, gaping holes below her waterline. Steam

pressure and electric power were lost almost immediately, and the ship lost headway. Oil poured out of her underwater wounds, and sea water poured in. Soon she was listing sharply to port. Gradually, the list increased until the inclinometer on the ship's bridge showed that she was tilted 26 degrees. It was difficult to walk on her sloping flight deck. Below decks, where the only light came from battery-powered battle lanterns, it was nearly impossible. With no power and no way to close the underwater holes in the ship's hull, there was nothing the damage-control crews could do to correct the dangerous list. And if it got worse, the giant ship might capsize, trapping her crew within her hull.

At a few minutes before 3:00, less than a half-hour

after the torpedoes had struck, Captain Buckmaster ordered his crew to abandon ship.

This was a sad duty for the captain. A veteran of almost 30 years in the Navy, Buckmaster had spent most of his career in battleships. But in 1936, recognizing the growing importance of naval aviation, he had learned to fly. He had been skipper of *Yorktown* since early 1941. He loved his ship, which he had fought so skillfully through the Battle of the Coral Sea. He had seen her quickly patched up at Pearl Harbor, and he had brought her safely through the fierce dive-bombing attack earlier in the day. Now, with the Battle of Midway nearly won, *Yorktown* had to admit defeat.

Yorktown planes that still were in the air headed for *Enterprise* and *Hornet*. Buckmaster made one last inspection of his doomed ship, to be sure no one was left aboard. Then he climbed down a rope to a waiting destroyer.

Only half the airmen who took off from *Hiryu* survived the attack. They returned to their carrier and told Admiral Yamaguchi that they, too, had sunk an American carrier.

15.

The Last of the Striking Force

A few minutes before noon, just before Kobayashi's attack, Admiral Fletcher had sent ten *Yorktown* SBDs on a search mission to the north and west. He believed that one Japanese carrier had escaped that morning's dive-bombing attack. He wanted to find that carrier and send her to the bottom.

At 2:45 P.M. Lieutenant Samuel Adams, piloting one of the scout planes, came upon *Hiryu* steaming north with two battleships, three cruisers, and four destroyers. They were about 110 miles west of *Yorktown*.

Fletcher had already shifted his flag to *Astoria* when the contact report came over the air. *Yorktown* was about to be abandoned. But Spruance was nearby with *Enterprise* and *Hornet*, neither of which had been hit. Spruance heard Adams' report and quickly signaled to Fletcher that he would attack. At 3:30 he launched two dozen SBDs from *Enterprise*. Eleven of them were armed with 1000-pound bombs. The rest carried two 500-pounders each. At a few minutes after four, *Hornet* launched 16 more dive bombers. They went without fighters, for none could be spared. Those that were left were needed for CAP.

Fourteen of the planes that took off from *Enterprise* were from *Yorktown's* air group. The *Yorktown* pilots had good reason to want to find *Hiryu*. The other ten were all that remained of *Enterprise's* two Dauntless squadrons, which once had numbered 38 planes. The rest of *Enterprise's* SBDs either had been shot down or were too badly damaged to fly again.

The *Enterprise* strike was commanded by Lieutenant Earl Gallaher, who had flown with Wade McClusky that morning. McClusky could not lead the attack himself. He was grounded with a shoulder wound which he had acquired that morning, when a Zero chased him partway back from the battle. Mechanics checking over his plane found that it had 58 bullet holes, and that the air-group commander had made it back with only two gallons of gas to spare.

Gallaher located what was left of Nagumo's Carrier Striking Force at 5 P.M. *Hiryu* and her escorts still were steaming north. Three columns of smoke on the southern horizon marked the spots where *Akagi, Kaga,* and *Soryu* were dying.

Since early morning, *Hiryu* had been attacked by more than 70 planes. Twenty-six torpedoes and 70 bombs had been aimed in her direction. That she was still afloat—and, in fact, had not even been scratched—was a tribute to Captain Tomeo Kaku's remarkable ship handling, the skill of her fighter pilots, and the poor marksmanship of some inexperienced Americans. *Hiryu* had just recovered the last of Tomonaga's

SBD Dauntless releasing a 500-pound bomb. The perforated strips of metal below the wings are dive brakes.

planes, and six fighters were patrolling overhead. Five dive bombers and four torpedo planes were on the deck. These 15 planes were all that remained of Nagumo's once-powerful 261-plane air armada.

Most of the carrier's dog-tired crew were below decks eating a quick supper of cold rice.

Admiral Yamaguchi believed that his two attacks on *Yorktown* had sunk two different carriers. He was planning to launch his few remaining planes to sink what he thought was the third and last American flattop just as soon as his pilots were fed and their planes readied for one more mission. A search plane was about to take off to look for Fletcher's "last" carrier.

At 5:03, just as *Hiryu* was getting ready to launch the scout, Gallaher gave the signal to dive. His SBDs were at 19,000 feet, attacking from the southwest. The sun, behind them, would make them hard to see from below. With luck they might take Yamaguchi by surprise.

But they were seen by a sharp-eyed lookout. Captain Kaku put his ship into a hard turn. The Zeros flying CAP began climbing to intercept the dive bombers. Anti-aircraft guns swung skyward and began to fire.

The Zeros climbed up past the diving SBDs, flipped into dives of their own, and came down on the bombers' tails, their 20-millimeter cannons spitting explosive shells. Rear-seat gunners fired back with their smaller machine guns. An SBD went out of control and fell toward the sea, leaving a long trail of black smoke. The others dove on. For once the Japanese fighters' speed gave them no advantage, for the Zeros could not dive slowly enough to keep from passing the dive bombers. After a quick diving pass, the Zeros had to break off and climb again in order to get another shot at the slower SBDs.

Captain Kaku's sudden turn threw off the aim of the first few pilots, and three bombs fell harmlessly into the sea. But the next four crashed through the flight deck and exploded, all of them near the carrier's island. One of the explosions blew the midships elevator out of its place in the flight deck and threw it up against the island. The wrecked elevator, standing on its edge, completely blocked the forward view from Captain Kaku's bridge. Meanwhile, fires broke out topside and below decks. Planes and ammunition exploded. Torrents of burning gasoline ran through bomb holes and down ladders. Suddenly proud *Hiryu*, the last of Nagumo's carriers, was a mass of roaring flames. The SBDs had scored again.

Damage-control parties did their best, but the fires could not be put out. By late evening, *Hiryu*'s engines had stopped turning and the ship was drifting help-lessly. Two desperate efforts were made to send dam-age-control teams to the engine rooms, but both failed. The engines could not be started, and the men in the engine rooms were trapped. By this time water from fire hoses had filled so many compartments that the ship was beginning to list. Soon she was heeling over 15 degrees. At 2:30 in the morning, fearing that the ship might capsize, Admiral Yamaguchi ordered all hands to gather on the flight deck. Only 800 men, out of a crew of 1500, answered the call.

"As commander of this carrier division," the admiral told them, "I am responsible for the loss of *Hiryu* and *Soryu*. I shall remain on board to the end. I command all of you to leave the ship and continue your loyal service to His Majesty, the Emperor."

Yamaguchi's staff officers begged him to abandon ship with them so that he might fight again, but the admiral's mind was made up. Someone found a small cask of water, and the admiral asked his officers to join him in a toast to the Emperor and victory. Then he gave his cap to Commander Seiroku Ito, his chief of staff, and said farewell.

Captain Kaku also was determined to stay aboard. The two men watched their shipmates leave. Then they climbed back to the bridge and waited for death.

At 5:10 A.M., as the moon which Yamamoto had hoped would shine on the invasion of Midway was beginning to set, Japanese destroyers fired a pair of torpedoes into *Hiryu*'s hull. The ship could not be saved, and it would be better to see her sink than to let her fall into American hands. Then the remaining ships of the Striking Force steamed off, leaving the doomed carrier to her fate.

Hiryu did not go down immediately. Shortly after 7 A.M., a search plane from one of the Northern Force's light carriers reported that she still was afloat. Swooping low to get a closer look, the pilot saw several men moving about her decks. He radioed this information to Admiral Yamamoto, who immediately sent a destroyer to investigate. By the time the destroyer arrived, however, *Hiryu* had disappeared forever beneath the waves.

The sailors whom the scout pilot had seen also disappeared, at least as far as their countrymen were concerned. But they were picked up later by an American ship. They told their captors that they had been trapped in an engine room when *Hiryu* was abandoned. The Japanese torpedoes that sank the ship actually had saved their lives by blasting open an escape route. The sailors had found their way to the flight deck and stayed there, hopeful that they might be rescued. They apparently did not climb up to the bridge, for they did not mention seeing Admiral Yamaguchi or Captain Kaku. A few minutes after 8:00, when they were sure the ship was about to sink, they went over the side. They got away just in time to avoid being sucked under as *Hiryu* began her long, cold plunge to the bottom of the deep Pacific.

16.

The End of the Battle

On the battleship *Yamato*, 200 miles west of Nagumo's stricken carriers, Admiral Yamamoto and his staff spent the night of June 4 trying to make some sense out of the information they had received bit by bit during the day of furious fighting. Yamamoto was not at all pleased with Nagumo's performance. He was annoyed particularly now that the Striking Force commander failed to use his surface ships to press a night attack against the American carriers.

Neither Yamamoto nor Nagumo knew exactly how many American ships had been in the battle. At 4:14 P.M. Admiral Yamaguchi had radioed that his returning pilots reported three carriers, five cruisers, and 15 destroyers in the American task force. But the Japanese admirals believed that *Hiryu*'s pilots had sunk or badly damaged two of the American flat-tops. Then, about an hour before sunset, a scout plane from the cruiser *Chikuma* reported "four enemy carriers, six cruisers, and 15 destroyers, 30 miles east of the burning carrier." The pilot had seen *Enterprise* and *Hornet* steaming away from the burning *Yorktown*. With the two carriers were most of the cruisers and destroyers of the combined task force of Fletcher and Spruance. The pilot had counted the ships correctly, but he mistook two cruisers for carriers.

Yamamoto must have known that Nimitz could not have sent that many carriers to Midway. But whether the enemy had four carriers protected by six cruisers or one carrier protected by nine, Admiral Nagumo still had two big battleships, three cruisers, and 11 destroyers, all of them undamaged and all of them trained in night battle tactics. Moreover, Vice Admiral Kondo was steaming northward from his position with the Invasion Force with two more battleships, five cruisers, and eight destroyers, plus the light carrier *Zuiho* with 11 torpedo bombers and 12 fighters. With their four battleships, mounting a total of 32 14-inch guns, Nagumo and Kondo could have sunk the American carriers and cruisers in a night engagement without even coming within range of the American 8-inchers. The only real question was whether or not the battleships could catch Fletcher and Spruance before dawn, for the American task force was 100 miles east of Nagumo and apparently heading eastward.

And the battle would have to be joined before dawn, for at sunrise the advantage would shift back to the Americans as carrier-based planes and Midway's remaining aircraft once again took to the air.

At 9:30 P.M., however, Admiral Nagumo radioed that the enemy was steaming *west* with five carriers, six cruisers, and 15 destroyers, and that he himself was retiring to the northwest at 18 knots. Yamamoto promptly ordered Kondo to take command of the Striking Force, leaving Nagumo only the cruiser *Nagara,* which had rescued him from his flagship, and a few destroyers which were standing by the burning *Akagi* and *Hiryu.* Yamamoto guessed that Nagumo was too shaken by the loss of his carriers to be of further use in the battle. He probably was right.

Early that afternoon, Admiral Yamamoto himself had begun to steam directly toward the battle with the powerful Main Body. But he was 200 miles from Nagumo and a good 300 miles west of Fletcher and Spruance. There was fog between him and the battle. This would slow his progress, and his battleships would have to zigzag in order to be safe from submarine attack. It was almost certain that he would not be able to bring his big guns to bear on any American ships before midmorning. By that time, the battle probably would have been decided.

The Aleutian Screening Force, with the battleships and cruisers which Yamamoto had ordered to come back from the north, would rejoin Yamamoto at 9 A.M., still too far to the west of the battle area to be of any help. And the carriers *Ryujo* and *Junyo,* now steaming south from their position off the Aleutians, could not arrive before midafternoon.

Fletcher, meanwhile, had turned over tactical command to Spruance. At 3:30 in the afternoon, as *Enterprise* was launching her attack on *Hiryu,* Spruance had signaled to Fletcher:

A destroyer stands by the badly listing *Yorktown.*

DO YOU HAVE ANY INSTRUCTIONS FOR ME?

Fletcher signaled back:

NONE. I WILL CONFORM TO YOUR MOVEMENTS.

This made good sense, for Spruance's fighting team still was intact, and Spruance was commanding it from the well-equipped flag bridge of the carrier *Enterprise.* Fletcher, on the other hand, was now in a cruiser, which did not have the proper radio equipment for the commander of a carrier task force.

Spruance had no reports of Kondo's movements and could only guess where Yamamoto's battleships might be. But he knew as well as Yamamoto that the Japanese would have a tremendous advantage in a night gun duel. Leaving a single destroyer standing by *Yorktown,* with orders to sink her if necessary to prevent her capture, he led his force to the east for most of the night, hoping to avoid a night engagement. Shortly before dawn, he reversed his course and steamed to the west, to be in position for an air strike in the morning.

"I did not feel justified," he wrote in his battle report, "in risking a night encounter with possibly superior enemy forces, but on the other hand I did not want to be too far away from Midway the next morning. I wished to have a position from which either to follow up retreating enemy forces or to break up a landing attack on Midway."

At fifteen minutes after midnight Admiral Yamamoto decided that Kondo could not overtake the American task force before dawn. Rather than risk a daylight battle against superior air power, he began recalling his forces.

Yamamoto's staff officers, ashamed to face defeat, offered suggestions—but it was too late. In despair, one of them asked, "How can we apologize to His Majesty?"

Yamamoto quickly accepted full responsibility. "Leave that to me," he said. "I am the only one who must apologize to His Majesty."

At five minutes before 3:00 that morning—it was now June 5—Admiral Yamamoto canceled his Midway operation.

But the battle was not quite over. Just before Yamamoto admitted that he was beaten the American submarine *Tambor*, patrolling on the surface, sighted a group of ships on the horizon. Unable to tell whether they were enemy or friendly, Lieutenant Commander John Murphy, the submarine's skipper, decided to follow them.

The ships turned out to be the cruisers and destroyers of Admiral Kurita's Close Support Group, part of the Midway Invasion Force. Before Murphy had been shadowing them long, the submarine was spotted by a Japanese lookout. Admiral Kurita immediately ordered all ships to make an emergency turn, just in case the sub should have fired its torpedoes. In the confusion that followed, the cruisers *Mogami* and *Mikuma* collided. Both were badly damaged.

Murphy was unable to maneuver *Tambor* into position for a torpedo attack, but he reported the incident by radio. The next day planes from *Enterprise* and *Hornet* found the two crippled cruisers and sent *Mikuma* to the bottom. *Mogami* eventually made her way to the Japanese base at the island of Truk. But she was so badly damaged, first by the collision and then by repeated air attacks, that she was out of action for more than a year.

Yorktown stayed afloat all night. A boarding party went aboard her from the destroyer *Hughes* early the next morning. In midafternoon the listing hulk was taken in tow by the minesweeper *Vireo*, which Nimitz had ordered to the scene. Soon crewmen from a second destroyer were sent to help the *Hughes* salvage party. Then the little minesweeper headed for Pearl

Harbor at a snail's pace, hauling the huge carrier behind her, while the two destroyers circled to guard *Yorktown* from any Japanese submarines which might be lurking in the depths.

They steamed that way all night, a wounded giant being dragged by a midget, with two small warriors circling around them in the darkness. And again *Yorktown* remained afloat through the night.

The morning of June 6, the destroyer *Hammann* came alongside with a new salvage party, 170 officers and men who had volunteered to go back aboard with Captain Buckmaster and man the carrier until she could be brought safely to port. The destroyer made fast to the carrier's starboard side. With power from the destroyer's generators, the salvage crew pumped out enough water to begin correcting the carrier's list. Planes and other loose weights were pushed over the port side to lighten the ship and make it easier to keep her on an even keel. Several destroyers formed a circle, a mile from the carrier, watching and listening for enemy submarines. By noon all hands believed that *Yorktown* could be saved.

But *Yorktown* had fought her last battle. Already she had been spotted by a seaplane from one of Yamamoto's retiring cruisers. Now the Japanese admiral sent a submarine to destroy her.

Lieutenant Commander Tanabe, skipper of the submarine *I-168*, brought his boat close by at periscope depth shortly after noon, June 6. He took his time, skillfully avoiding the destroyers which were circling the carrier to prevent just this kind of attack. The destroyers had sonar—underwater listening gear—and trained crews to operate it, but oil and debris in the water may have interfered with the sound waves so that they failed to reach the submarine and bounce back to the sensitive microphones aboard the destroyers. Whatever the explanation, at 1:30 P.M. *I-168* was in firing position, less than a mile off *Yorktown*'s starboard side. The carrier made an easy target, moving at only two or three knots. Tanabe fired a spread of four torpedoes from his forward tubes and left his periscope up to watch the result.

Gunners on the destroyer *Hammann* saw the torpedoes approaching. Desperately, they tried to explode them with 20-millimeter gunfire. They had no luck. Most of the shells bounced off the surface of the sea. None penetrated deep enough to hit the torpedoes.

One torpedo ran wild and missed the target. One was too shallow and hit *Hammann* amidships, breaking her back. The others passed under the destroyer and exploded against *Yorktown*'s starboard side, far below the waterline. Because of her port list, they hit below her belt of heavy armor plate.

American destroyers immediately began a fierce depth-charge attack on the Japanese submarine. Tanabe later claimed to have counted 60 explosions close aboard. He dove to 200 feet, determined to survive. The attack went on for several minutes, every explosion buffeting the submarine, knocking her crew to the deck, and loosening fittings throughout the boat. The lights went out, and deadly chlorine gas began to seep aft from the forward battery room. Then the attack ended, just as suddenly as it had begun. Taking a desperate chance, Tanabe decided to come up for air.

Once on the surface, the submarine skipper saw the American destroyers some distance away. To his discomfort they also saw him, came about, and began to close in, guns blazing. Reluctantly Tanabe gave the order to dive again. This time he reversed course and headed directly for the pursuing destroyers. They passed directly over him at high speed, and he kept going in the opposite direction. When he surfaced again, he was alone. He stayed on the surface long enough to recharge his batteries and get some fresh air in the boat, and then he headed for home.

Yorktown and *Hammann* were not so lucky. *Hammann* went down in less than five minutes. More than 80 of her 250-man crew went with her. Some were trapped aboard. Some were killed by the torpedo explosion. Still others were killed when her own depth charges and one of her boilers exploded under water. Another 85 *Hammann* crewmen were injured.

For a while it looked as though *Yorktown* still might be saved. Efforts to keep her afloat continued for the rest of the afternoon and part of the night. Since the new torpedo wounds were in her starboard side, the water rushing in actually helped to correct the port list. But the big ship settled deeper and deeper as she

Hammann's bow disappearing minutes after the destroyer was hit by a Japanese torpedo. Many of the crew were trapped aboard. The photograph was made from a nearby American warship, probably *Yorktown*.

took on more and more sea water. During the night, the tons of water in the ship's innards shifted to port, and suddenly she once again took on a dangerous list. Once again, Captain Buckmaster had to admit that she could not be saved. Again, he sadly gave the order to abandon ship.

About 6 A.M. on June 7, the port side of her flight deck almost awash, *Yorktown* slowly began to capsize. Aircraft in the hangar deck, furniture in compartments below decks, and all manner of loose gear throughout the ship began to slide to port with a grinding roar that could be heard on the destroyers nearby. The added weight on her low side tipped her still further.

Yorktown men aboard the destroyers manned the rails for a last look at the ship that had been their home, unashamed of the tears in their eyes. Destroyers half-masted their colors and all hands stood at attention as the great ship rolled over and disappeared beneath the oily sea.

The Battle of Midway was over.

Wounded survivors of *Yorktown* being transferred from the cruiser *Portland* (right) to the submarine tender *Fulton*, which came out from Pearl Harbor to get them from the overcrowded cruiser.

Avenger

17.

Why?

Why did it happen? Why did Admiral Yamamoto, one of the greatest naval leaders of all time, suffer such a costly defeat at the hands of a much weaker enemy?

Yamamoto entered the Battle of Midway with:

  8 aircraft carriers
  11 battleships
  24 cruisers
  58 destroyers
  20 submarines
  and a large number of transports and other auxiliaries.

No admiral before, and few since, ever commanded such a powerful armada. Yet Yamamoto was beaten by an American force consisting of only:

  3 carriers
  0 battleships
  8 cruisers
  17 destroyers
  19 submarines
  and a few oilers.

Mikuma after the June 5 attack by bombers from *Hornet* and *Enterprise*. The Japanese cruiser sank that night.

(Nimitz had five more cruisers and a few more destroyers, submarines, and seaplane tenders in Admiral Theobald's Aleutian Force, but they took no part in the battle.)

Admiral Yamamoto set out to do two things: capture Midway and destroy the U.S. Pacific Fleet. He failed to do either. Admiral Nimitz, on the other hand, ordered his commanders to prevent the capture of Midway and to do as much damage as possible to the Japanese Combined Fleet without exposing their own forces more than necessary. They succeeded in both tasks.

In losing the battle, Yamamoto also lost four big carriers and the heavy cruiser *Mikuma*, 322 aircraft, and more than 3000 officers and men. All the planes of Nagumo's four big carriers, ten seaplanes from battleships and cruisers, and about 50 land planes, which the carriers were ferrying to Midway for later use by the Japanese occupation forces, went to the bottom. The Japanese dead included a rear admiral (Yamaguchi), the captains of three aircraft carriers, and about a hundred of Japan's best pilots, as well as other officers and highly trained enlisted men.

Nimitz lost a carrier and a destroyer, 147 aircraft (most of them carrier planes), and 307 officers and men. These losses hurt, but they were small compared to Yamamoto's. And more than a third of the American planes shot down were Devastator torpedo planes, Buffalo fighters, and Vindicator dive bombers, obsolete types which would have been scrapped within a few months anyway.

Yamamoto had more ships, more men, more planes, more guns, and more torpedoes—more of everything needed to win the battle. As the attacker, he alone chose the time and place of the engagement. Most of his pilots were more experienced than most American carrier pilots. And there is no question that the Japanese airmen were brave. Fliers like Joichi Tomonaga and Michio Kobayashi, who died leading the two air attacks against *Yorktown*, were as devoted to their country and as brave in the face of danger as men like Waldron and Henderson. Genuine heroes fought on both sides.

By all odds Yamamoto should have won the battle. Why, then, did he lose? What made the difference between victory and defeat?

Four major factors played a part in the American victory—intelligence, strategy, tactics, and luck.

Intelligence, knowledge of the enemy's plans and his movements, probably was the most important.

In the years before and during World War II, Japan was a nation of mystery. The Imperial Army controlled the entire country. Little news was allowed to leak out, either to the Japanese public or to the rest of the world. Yet, in spite of Japan's passion for secrecy, Admiral Nimitz knew far more about Yamamoto's plans for the Battle of Midway than Yamamoto knew about the movements of the U.S. Pacific Fleet. Credit for this must go to American intelligence officers who cracked Japan's secret codes, and to other officers and men who spent long, tiresome days listening to Japanese radio messages, and translating and decoding them.

These men gave Admiral Nimitz vital information. Nimitz was a brilliant strategist. He might have guessed what Yamamoto was up to, even without this help. But the work of men like Commander Rochefort, who proved before the battle that the letters "AF" in Japanese radio messages meant Midway, made it possible for Nimitz to be sure. These officers and men, who took no part in the actual fighting, had a lot to do with winning the battle.

If he had not known something of Yamamoto's plans, Admiral Nimitz would not have had *Enterprise* and *Hornet* in position to counterattack when Nagumo struck Midway. If he had not known that a major battle was in the offing, he probably would not have brought *Yorktown* back to Pearl Harbor immediately after the Battle of the Coral Sea, insisting that the Pearl Harbor Navy Yard repair her in record time. And without these three carriers, Midway would have been almost completely unprotected.

Because he had been warned of Yamamoto's plans, Nimitz recognized that the Aleutian attack was a feint. If Nimitz had sent his carriers north to repel that attack, Fletcher and Spruance might have sunk a few ships in the cold North Pacific, but Yamamoto would have captured Midway almost without opposition. Then the U.S. Pacific Fleet would have had to fight off attacks from land-based planes, as well as the planes from Nagumo's carriers, and Yamamoto's complicated battle plan might have been carried out successfully.

The Japanese, on the other hand, seemed to ignore the importance of intelligence at almost every level of command. The Japanese Naval General Staff accepted a wholly inaccurate intelligence estimate. It included the wild guess that a strong American task force was operating in the South Pacific, near the Solomon Islands. No effort was made to confirm this information. Instead, the estimate was passed to Yamamoto. The Japanese also believed that *Yorktown* had been sunk in the Battle of the Coral Sea. A few reconnaissance flights the morning after that battle would have shown that this was not so.

Perhaps these bad guesses were due, in part, to overconfidence. They also helped build more overconfidence—what one Japanese naval officer, writing after the war, called the "victory disease" which infected all levels of Japanese command.

Perhaps this is why the Japanese Commander in Chief was not too concerned when Operation K, the plan to reconnoiter Pearl Harbor with seaplanes flying from French Frigate Shoals, failed to work out. With *Yorktown* on the bottom and most of the remaining ships of Nimitz's fleet in the South Pacific, Yamamoto would have little to fear. But if Yamamoto's master plan had included some alternate way to steal a look at Pearl Harbor, just in case the French Frigate Shoals plan should fail, he might have learned where the U.S. Pacific Fleet's carriers really were. Instead, he abandoned the idea, and he was so confident of victory that he did not even bother to warn Nagumo that the reconnaissance plan had not been carried out.

Admiral Yamamoto's choice of strategy will always be a mystery. He may have been right in trying to force the U.S. Pacific Fleet to fight before it had completely recovered from Pearl Harbor, and before the hundreds of ships being built by American industry could be readied for battle. But there was no need for such a complicated battle plan. Yamamoto's fleet was so much larger and so much more powerful than anything Nimitz could muster that he did not have to try so hard to surprise and confuse his American enemies. Surprise can play an important part in naval strategy, but it is more of a help to the side with the weaker forces than to the stronger warrior. In relying so completely on surprise, Yamamoto ignored a more important principle—concentration of force. In an effort to trick Nimitz, he weakened his own fleet by scattering it all over the Pacific.

The Aleutian feint was nearly useless. The capture of barren outposts like Kiska and Attu could have no great effect on the outcome of the war. The only real result of this operation was to deprive Admiral Nagumo of two small carriers, four battleships, nine cruisers, and 12 destroyers, which he could have used to good advantage off Midway.

Yamamoto kept another small carrier between 200 and 300 miles west of the action, tied to his own Main Body of battleships and cruisers. He assigned a fourth light carrier to Admiral Kondo's Midway Invasion Force. If these small carriers had been under Nagumo's command, the Striking Force commander would have had four more flight decks and about 52 more Zeros, 19 more torpedo planes, and another 42 dive bombers. Instead, all four small carriers and their more than 100 planes were out of range when Nagumo was in trouble.

Nagumo could have used more than just the carriers. He could have made good use of the scout planes and anti-aircraft guns of the battleships, cruisers, and destroyers assigned to the Midway Invasion Force, the Aleutian Force, and Yamamoto's Main Body. In addition, the big guns of these ships and the torpedo tubes of the cruisers and destroyers would have made

a lot of difference if Yamamoto had been able to move
them into position for a night surface attack on the
American fleet.

But Admiral Yamamoto did not make all the Japanese mistakes. Vice Admiral Nagumo made his share.
Yamamoto's errors were errors of strategy—mistakes
in the overall planning of the whole operaton. Nagumo's mistakes were errors in tactics—bad decisions
made just before and during the battle.

Perhaps Yamamoto was unwise to give Nagumo two
missions, but Nagumo also made the error of forgetting
which of the two was more important. He was right to
attack Midway the morning of June 4, but he seemed
to forget that the whole purpose of this attack was to
force a fleet action. He certainly should have ordered
a more thorough search for American ships that morning. When two of his search planes were delayed in
taking off, he should have replaced them immediately
with other planes, even if he had to borrow them from
the second strike he was holding in reserve.

Nagumo made another error in judgment when he
ordered *Akagi* and *Kaga* to rearm their torpedo planes
with bombs for a second strike against Midway when
he was not certain that there were no American ships
within range. Even if he believed that the second
strike was needed, he should have kept torpedoes on
enough of his Kates to attack whatever enemy ships
his scouts might find. His scouts *did* find *Yorktown*,
but by the time they had identified her most of
Nagumo's torpedo planes were armed with bombs.

Nagumo's most dangerous mistake was delaying his attack on *Yorktown,* once his scout reported that the American task force did include a carrier. True, he could not have put a perfectly balanced attack force into the air immediately. He could not even have given his dive bombers much fighter cover. But at that point it was more important to attack with whatever he could launch than to wait until he could muster a full attack wave of dive bombers, torpedo planes, and fighters.

He made another serious tactical error when he formed Tomonaga's first attack wave. He used dive bombers from *Akagi* and *Kaga,* torpedo bombers from *Hiryu* and *Soryu,* and fighters from all four carriers. By having all four carriers launch at once, he saved some time getting the attack wave into the air, but at that moment time was not too important. But because planes from all four carriers were in the air, all four flight decks were tied up in recovery operations when Tomonaga returned a few hours later. And then time really was important. If Nagumo had ordered only two of his carriers to provide all the planes for Tomonaga's strike against Midway, the other two would have been free to attack *Yorktown* the moment the seaplane pilot reported that the American ships were "accompanied by what appears to be an aircraft carrier." Then a powerful strike would have been on its way before the American carrier planes found Nagumo's Striking Force and disabled three of his four carriers.

Until the Battle of Midway, Nagumo had had a brilliant career. He had commanded a cruiser and a battleship, and served on the Naval General Staff. By 1941, however, when he had reached the grade of vice admiral and was commanding a carrier striking fleet, he seemed to have slowed down. He had become less decisive and often left many important decisions to the officers of his staff. As often was the case with senior Japanese admirals, he confined his attention to the most important policy matters, and tended to remain aloof from day-to-day decisions. Thus he may have been out of the habit of making quick decisions. His performance in the Battle of Midway surely shows him to have been indecisive at a time when quick decisions, and correct decisions, were needed to save the day.

Luck, too, played an important part in the battle. It always does. Luck gave Spruance the opportunity to catch Nagumo when his carriers' flight decks were jammed with planes low on gas and out of ammunition. By luck Wade McClusky, having missed Nagumo's carriers, just happened to see the destroyer *Arashi* steaming toward the Carrier Striking Force.

But a skillful commander makes his own luck. While luck may have provided the opportunities, Fletcher, Spruance, McClusky, and other American commanders were quick to grasp them. At Midway the Americans took advantage of almost every break in the game. The Japanese did not.

The American victory, therefore, was due not just to Japanese mistakes and to luck. Chester Nimitz adopted sound strategy, instructed his task-force commanders thoroughly and wisely, and then left them a free hand to pick their own tactics. They made wise decisions. Their orders were carried out brilliantly by carrier captains, air-group commanders, and individual fliers, who ignored the odds and pressed home their attacks until the enemy ships were in flames.

The Battle of Midway was a victory of intelligence, strategy, tactics, and luck. It also was a victory of bravery and sacrifice.

Midway was a turning point. Yamamoto had planned that it would be one. And Yamamoto must take most

After the Battle of Midway, Admiral Nimitz presents medals to *Enterprise* aviators. In the background are ships sunk and damaged at Pearl Harbor by Japanese carrier planes just six months before.

of the blame for the fact that at Midway the war turned against Japan. As Commander in Chief of the Japanese Combined Fleet, Yamamoto had proposed the eastward offensive. The operation plan was his, and he commanded the fleet that carried it out. So few other officers were consulted in advance that even Nagumo and Kondo were not told of the plan until just a few weeks before the fleet sailed.

It was Yamamoto who scattered the Japanese fleet all over the ocean, and it was he who deprived his Striking Force commander of carriers, scout planes, and gunfire support he so sorely needed. It was Yamamoto, indeed, who owed the Emperor an apology for the bitter defeat.

The truth about the Battle of Midway was kept from the Japanese people until after the war. The battle was called a victory, and official reports were labeled "top secret." Even high-ranking officers of the Japanese Army and Navy were not told the full story of the defeat. Wounded officers and sailors were hidden away in special hospital rooms. Even their families were not allowed to visit them. The Japanese high command refused to admit publicly that Japan could be beaten.

But secrecy could not change the facts. After Midway there never was any question who would win the war for the Pacific. The only real questions were when the war would end, and how many lives would be the price of victory.

Epilogue

The name *Yorktown* was assigned to a new carrier being built at Newport News, Virginia. She was launched January 21, 1943, and was still in commission 25 years later. *Hornet* was sunk by Japanese dive bombers in the Battle of Santa Cruz, October 26, 1942. A new *Hornet* was launched at Newport News August 30, 1943. As this is written, she too still serves in the U.S. Fleet.

Enterprise survived the war and was decommissioned at Bayonne, New Jersey, on February 17, 1947. Twelve years later, the great ship was scrapped. She was too old and had gone through too many battles to fight again. But a new *Enterprise* joined the fleet in 1962. More than 1000 feet long and powered by nuclear reactors instead of oil, she is a fitting namesake for the "Big E" of World War II.

Admiral Yamamoto continued in his post as Commander in Chief of the Japanese Combined Fleet until his death April 18, 1943. A bomber in which he was a passenger was shot down by U.S. Army Air Corps fighter planes in the Solomon Islands. His ashes were returned to Tokyo for a state funeral. Yamamoto's flagship, the battleship *Yamato*, was sunk by U.S. Navy planes off Okinawa on April 7, 1945.

Chester W. Nimitz was promoted to the grade of Fleet Admiral in December 1944, and remained in command of the U.S. Pacific Fleet and the Pacific Ocean Area until the end of the war. He represented the United States at the ceremony aboard USS *Missouri* in Tokyo Bay on September 2, 1945, when Japan formally surrendered. He later served for two years as Chief of Naval Operations, the highest post in the U.S. Navy, and was an adviser to the Secretary of the Navy until his death, at the age of 82, in early 1967.

That same year, the Navy began construction of its second nuclear-powered aircraft carrier. Before the keel was laid, the Navy Department announced that the world's most modern warship would be named USS *Nimitz*.

Japanese Combined Fleet
(Admiral Yamamoto)

Main Body (Admiral Yamamoto in YAMATO)
- 3 battleships: YAMATO, NAGATO, MUTSU
- 1 light carrier: HOSHO (8 Kate torpedo bombers)
- 1 destroyer
- 2 seaplane carriers (carrying midget submarines instead of seaplanes)

Main Body Screen (Rear Admiral Hashimoto in SENDAI)
- 1 light cruiser: SENDAI
- 12 destroyers

Aleutian Screening Force (Vice Admiral Takasu in HYUGA)
- 4 battleships: HYUGA, ISE, FUSO, YAMASHIRO
- 2 light cruisers: OI, KITAKAMI

Supply Unit
- 4 fleet oilers

First Carrier Striking Force (Vice Admiral Nagumo)
Carrier Division One (Vice Admiral Nagumo in AKAGI)
- 2 carriers: AKAGI (21 Zero fighters, 21 Kate torpedo bombers, 21 Val dive bombers), KAGA (21 Zeros, 30 Kates, 21 Vals)

Carrier Division Two (Rear Admiral Yamaguchi in HIRYU)
- 2 carriers: HIRYU (21 Zeros, 21 Kates, 21 Vals), SORYU (21 Zeros, 21 Kates, 21 Vals)

Support Group (Rear Admiral Abe in TONE)
- 2 battleships: HARUNA, KIRISHIMA
- 2 heavy cruisers: TONE, CHIKUMA

Screening Group (Rear Admiral Kimura in NAGARA)
- 1 light cruiser: NAGARA
- 11 destroyers: including ARASHI

Supply Unit
    1 destroyer
    5 fleet oilers

Midway Invasion Force (Vice Admiral Kondo)

Invasion Force Covering Group (Vice Admiral
Kondo in ATAGO)
    2 battleships: KONGO, HIEI
    1 light carrier: ZUIHO (12 fighters, 11 torpedo bombers)
    4 heavy cruisers: ATAGO, CHOKAI, MYOKO, HAGURO
    1 light cruiser: YURA
    8 destroyers
    4 fleet oilers
    1 repair ship

Close Support Group (Vice Admiral Kurita
in KUMANO)
    4 heavy cruisers: SUZUYA, KUMANO, MOGAMI, MIKUMA
    2 destroyers
    1 fleet oiler

Transport Group (Rear Admiral Tanaka
in JINTSU)
    15 transports (including 3 destroyer-transports), with
    5000 troops
    1 light cruiser: JINTSU
    10 destroyers
    1 fleet oiler: AKEBONO MARU

Seaplane Tender Group (Rear Admiral Fujita)
    2 seaplane carriers (24 fighter seaplanes, 8 scout planes)
    1 destroyer
    1 patrol boat

Minesweeper Group (Captain Miyamoto)
    4 minesweepers
    3 submarine chasers
    3 supply ships

Northern Force (Vice Admiral Hosogaya)

Northern Force Main Body (Vice Admiral
Hosogaya in NACHI)
    1 heavy cruiser: NACHI
    2 destroyers

Second Carrier Striking Force (Rear Admiral Kakuta in RYUJO)
2 light carriers: RYUJO (16 Zeros, 21 Vals), JUNYO (24 Zeros, 21 Vals)
2 heavy cruisers: MAYA, TAKAO
3 destroyers

Attu Invasion Force (Rear Admiral Omori in ABUKUMA)
1 light cruiser: ABUKUMA
4 destroyers
1 minelayer
1 transport, with 1200 troops

Kiska Invasion Force (Captain Ono in KISO)
2 light cruisers: KISO, TAMA
1 auxiliary cruiser: ASAKA MARU
3 destroyers
3 minesweepers
2 transports, with 1250 troops

Patrol and Reconnaissance Group (Rear Admiral Yamazaki)
5 submarines

Submarine Force (Vice Admiral Komatsu in KATORI at Kwajalein)
1 light cruiser: KATORI
2 submarine tenders
15 submarines, including I-168

Shore-Based Naval Air Force (Vice Admiral Tsukahara)
24 seaplanes
10 land-based bombers
72 torpedo planes
100 or more fighters

U.S. Pacific Fleet
(Admiral Nimitz at Pearl Harbor)

Carrier Striking Force (Rear Admiral Fletcher)
Task Force 17 (Rear Admiral Fletcher
in YORKTOWN)
1 carrier: YORKTOWN (25 F4F Wildcat fighters, 13 TBD Devastator torpedo bombers, 37 SBD Dauntless dive bombers)

Cruiser-Destroyer Screen (Rear Admiral Smith in ASTORIA)
2 heavy cruisers: ASTORIA, PORTLAND
6 destroyers: including HUGHES and HAMMANN

Task Force 16 (Rear Admiral Spruance
in ENTERPRISE)
2 carriers: ENTERPRISE (27 F4F, 14 TBD, 38 SBD), HORNET (27 F4F, 15 TBD, 37 SBD)

Cruiser-Destroyer Screen (Rear Admiral Kinkaid in NEW ORLEANS)
5 heavy cruisers: NEW ORLEANS, MINNEAPOLIS, VINCENNES, NORTHAMPTON, PENSACOLA
1 light cruiser: ATLANTA
9 destroyers

Oiler Group
2 fleet oilers
2 destroyers

**Submarine Force (Rear Admiral English
at Pearl Harbor)**
19 submarines: including NAUTILUS and TAMBOR

**Aleutian Force, Task Force 8
(Rear Admiral Theobald)**
Main Body (Rear Admiral Theobald in NASHVILLE)
2 heavy cruisers: INDIANAPOLIS, LOUISVILLE
3 light cruisers: NASHVILLE, ST. LOUIS, HONOLULU
4 destroyers

Air Search Group (Captain Gehres
at Dutch Harbor)
   3 seaplane tenders
   20 PBY Catalina seaplanes
   1 Army Air Corps B-17 Flying Fortress

Surface Search Group (Captain Parker at Kodiak)
   1 gunboat
   14 small patrol craft
   5 Coast Guard cutters
   1 fleet oiler

Army Air Corps Striking Group
(Brigadier General Butler at Kodiak)
   47 bombers
   109 fighters (at Cold Bay, Umnak, Otter Point, Kodiak,
   and Anchorage)

Destroyer Striking Group
   9 destroyers

Submarine Group
   6 submarines

Tanker Group
   2 fleet oilers
   1 merchant tanker

Forces at Midway (Captain Simard)
   32 PBY-5 and PBY-5A Catalina seaplanes and amphibious patrol bombers
   6 TBF Avenger torpedo bombers

Marine Aircraft Group 22
(Lieutenant Colonel Kimes)
   7 F4F Wildcats ⎱ Fighter Squadron 221 (Major Parks)
   20 F2A Buffalos ⎰
   16 SBD Dauntless ⎱ Scout Bomber Squadron 241
   11 SB2U Vindicators ⎰ (Major Henderson)

Army Air Corps Detachment
(Lieutenant Colonel Sweeney)
   4 B-26 Marauder medium bombers
   18 B-17 Flying Fortress long-range bombers

Sixth Marine Defense Battalion (Colonel Shannon)
    1200 troops

Motor Torpedo Boat Squadron 1
    8 PT boats at Midway
    2 PT boats at Kure
    4 small patrol craft at Midway

Miscellaneous (at French Frigate Shoals and nearby atolls)
    2 seaplane tenders
    1 destroyer
    1 oiler
    1 minesweeper
    1 converted yacht
    4 converted tuna fishing boats

Table of Aircraft Characteristics

Type	Name	Dimensions (feet)		Top speed (knots)	Typical ranges (nautical miles, speeds in knots)
		Wings	Length		
Japan					
Fighter	Mitsubishi Zero	40	30	285	685 at 210 kts. 890 at 150 kts.
Dive bomber	Aichi Type 99 Val	48	35	210	870 at 155 kts. 1085 at 115 kts.
Torpedo bomber	Nakajima Type 97 Kate	51	35	195	920 at 145 kts. 1060 at 115 kts.
United States					
Fighter	F2A Buffalo	35	26	275	700 at 205 kts. 835 at 140 kts.
Fighter	F4F Wildcat	38	29	285	640 at 215 kts. 750 at 130 kts.
Dive bomber	SBD Dauntless	42	33	220	710 at 160 kts. 745 at 125 kts.
Dive bomber	SB2U Vindicator	42	34	190	600 at 145 kts. 725 at 130 kts.
Torpedo bomber	TBF Avenger	54	41	240	665 at 180 kts. 785 at 145 kts.
Torpedo bomber	TBD Devastator	50	35	170	345 at 130 kts. 385 at 110 kts.
Patrol bomber	PBY Catalina	104	64	175	1390 at 130 kts. 1700 at 100 kts.

NOTE: Top speed is at best altitude (usually 14,000 to 16,000 feet). Ranges are at an average of approximately 75% and 60%

Armament		Side View
Guns	**Bombs**	
two 7.7-mm two 20-mm	2 (small)	
three 7.7-mm	800 lbs.	
three 7.7-mm	550 lbs. or 1 torpedo	
four .50-cal.	200 lbs.	
six .50-cal.	200 lbs.	
two .50-cal. one .30-cal.	1000 lbs.	
two .50-cal. two .30-cal.	1000 lbs.	
three .50-cal. one .30-cal.	1600 lbs. or 1 torpedo	
one .50-cal. one .30-cal.	1200 lbs. or 1 torpedo	
two .50-cal. two .30-cal.	4000 lbs. or 2 torpedoes	

of maximum speed, with full load, at best altitude. One knot =
1.15 mph.

Pronunciation of Japanese Names

No system of writing Japanese in our alphabet can represent all Japanese sounds perfectly, but readers will come close to the correct pronunciation if they will follow these rules:

(1) Pronounce consonants as in English.

(2) Pronounce vowels as in Italian or Spanish—*a* as in father; *e* like the *ay* sound in day; *i* like the double *e* in meet; *o* as in no; and *u* like the double *o* in boot.

(3) Pronounce all vowels. Admiral Abe's name is pronounced "ah-bay" rather than "abe" as in "Honest Abe."

(4) Try to pronounce all syllables of a Japanese word with approximately the same amount of stress rather than accenting a single syllable as in most other languages. If you can say "ee-so-ro-koo yah-mah-mo-to" (*not* "EE-so-RO-koo YAH-mah-MO-to"), you've got the idea.

Bibliography and Acknowledgments

The following books and pamphlets were consulted in the preparation of this book:

Frank, Pat, and Joseph D. Harrington. *Rendezvous at Midway: U.S.S. Yorktown and the Japanese Carrier Fleet*. New York: John Day, 1967.

Fuchida, Mitsuo, and Masatake Okumiya. *Midway: The Battle That Doomed Japan*. Annapolis: U.S. Naval Institute, 1955.

Halsey, William F., and J. Bryan, III. *Admiral Halsey's Story*. New York: McGraw-Hill, 1947.

Heinl, Robert D., Jr. *Marines at Midway*. U.S. Government Printing Office, 1948.

Jane's Fighting Ships, 1941 edition. New York: Macmillan, 1942.

Morison, Samuel Eliot. *History of United States Naval Operations in World War II*. Boston: Little, Brown, 1962.

Office of Naval Intelligence. *Combat Narratives: The Battle of Midway*. U.S. Government Printing Office, 1946.

Office of Naval Intelligence. *The Japanese Story of the Battle of Midway*. U.S. Government Printing Office, 1947.

Okumiya, Masatake, and Joro Horikoshi, with Martin Caidin. *Zero: The Inside Story of Japan's Air War in the Pacific*. New York: Ballantine Books, 1957.

Potter, E. B., and Chester W. Nimitz. *The Great Sea War: The Story of Naval Action in World War II*. Englewood Cliffs, N. J.: Prentice-Hall, 1960.

Potter, John Deane. *Yamamoto: The Man Who Menaced America.* New York: Viking Press, 1965.

Smith, William W. *Midway: Turning Point of the Pacific.* New York: Thomas Y. Crowell, 1966.

Stafford, Edward P. *The Big E: The Story of the USS Enterprise.* New York: Random House, 1962.

Taylor, Theodore. *The Magnificent Mitscher.* New York: W. W. Norton, 1954.

Toland, John. *But Not in Shame: The Six Months After Pearl Harbor.* New York: Random House, 1961.

Tuleja, Thaddeus V. *Climax at Midway.* New York: W. W. Norton, 1960.

U.S. Strategic Bombing Survey, Naval Analysis Division. *Campaigns of the Pacific War.* U.S. Government Printing Office, 1946.

U.S. Strategic Bombing Survey, Naval Analysis Division. *Interrogation of Japanese Officials.* U.S. Government Printing Office, 1946.

Of these sources, Fuchida and Okumiya's *Midway: The Battle That Doomed Japan* and Tuleja's *Climax at Midway* are particularly recommended for readers of Landmark Books who would like to know more about this fascinating battle. Walter Lord's *Incredible Victory* (New York: Harper & Row, 1967), which was published after this manuscript was completed and is therefore not listed above as a source, also is recommended highly.

When an event involves thousands of people and lasts for several days, eyewitness accounts almost always vary. Thus it is that in the many firsthand accounts of the Battle of Midway there are differences on numerous minor points—the exact number of aircraft aboard a particular carrier or in a particular attack formation, for example, or the exact time of an attack. On one important question—whether the Japanese carrier *Kaga* was sunk by Lieutenant Commander Leslie's *Yorktown* dive bombers or by *Enterprise* planes led by Lieutenant Commander McClusky—eminent naval historians disagree. An author must study such conflicting versions, compromise among them where compromise is possible, and rely on his own judgment where it is not. When all is done, he believes his version to be the closest to the truth, and if it is not he alone is to blame.

The author is indebted to the Office of Naval History and particularly to the Navy Department Library; the Adjutant General's Army Library in the Pentagon; the National Archives; and both the Pictorial Division and the Magazine and Book Division of the Office of the Assistant Secretary of Defense (Public Affairs).

Index

About the Author

Captain Edmund L. Castillo, USN, is the author of *The Seabees of World War II* (a Landmark Book) and *All About the U.S. Navy*. As a junior officer during World War II, he served aboard an attack cargo ship in the Pacific and later commanded two small amphibious ships. Some years after the war, he returned to the Pacific with the Seventh Fleet and to Japan with the Navy's Far East Headquarters. He also has served with the U.S. Sixth Fleet in the Mediterranean and at various shore stations. He is now chief of the Pentagon's press room.

He has degrees from Northwestern and Boston Universities. Enrolled in the Naval ROTC at Northwestern and commissioned on graduation, he transferred to the regular Navy in 1946. Captain Castillo and his wife live near Washington, D.C., with their three teen-age children, all of whom are veteran travelers.